THE GREAT INVITATION

Examining the Use of the Altar Call
in Evangelism

Erroll Hulse

AUDUBON PRESS
2601 Audubon Drive / P.O. Box 8055
Laurel, MS 39441-8000   USA

Orders: 800-405-3788
Inquiries: 601-649-8572
Voice: 601-649-8570 / Fax: 601-649-8571
E-mail: buybooks@audubonpress.com
Web Page: www.audubonpress.com

Original Edition:
Copyright 1986 Evangelical Press, Welwyn, Hertfordshire, England
Typeset by Inset, Cahpppel, Essex, England
Printed in Great Britain by The Bath Press, Avon

Cover design by Crisp Graphics

ISBN # 0-9742365-3-5

Unless otherwise stated, Scripture references are from the New
International Version, Hodder & Stoughton, 1979.

Contents

Acknowledgements

First and foremost I express my gratitude to our great Emmanuel for the means necessary for a writing ministry. The consistent help of an efficient and dedicated wife together with the sympathy of an excellent church have been invaluable. Particular appreciation is expressed for the assistance given by Don Stephens of Liverpool. He spent many hours giving helpful general assistance. John Legg of Northallerton has lent his discerning mind to the manuscript and his suggestions have been highly valued. Doreen Slegg of Sussex has always been willing to decipher my writing and type new drafts. Normally I do not express gratitude in this way because of reluctance to involve others where controversial matters are concerned. However, it is important that we testify of our dependence on the body of support that the Lord graciously provides and wherever there is anything profitable to ascribe the praise to him.

Several American pastors who have had a long experience of the invitation system have helped me with advice, but the issue is one so delicate that understandably they are not yet ready to stand up and be counted!

Endorsements

The notion that sinners can secure their own salvation by a "decision" is fraught with all kinds of theological mischief. It has reduced faith to bare intellectual assent, populated the church with people who have never even been convicted about their sin, and made public invitations into the same kind of sacramental indulgences the original Protestants repudiated. Errol Hulse has given a thorough biblical answer to this error, and I'm glad to see it back in print.

— **John MacArthur** is the pastor-teacher of *Grace Community Church* in Sun Valley, California, and president of The Master's College and Seminary.

Erroll Hulse's classic work is a biblical and balanced answer to modern decisionalism. Hulse shows from Scripture that there is a legitimate place for the ambassador of Christ to exhort sinners to be reconciled to God, to reason passionately with them from Scripture, to invite them to drink freely of the water of life, and to plead with them and beseech them to turn to the Savior. But he also stresses that regeneration is the work of the Holy Spirit to produce faith in the sinner, not a result of the sinner's independent "decision." The two ideas are perfectly harmonious, because our passionate preaching is the means by which God sovereignly and effectually calls the elect to himself.

— **Phil Johnson** is the Executive Director of *Grace to You*, a pastor at *Grace Community Church* in Sun Valley, California, and the Curator of *The Spurgeon Archive*.

My sincere thanks to Audubon Press for making Erroll Hulse's excellent book, The Great Invitation, *available again after twenty years since its original publication. It's this very kind of book that needs to be published again and read widely by evangelicals. The reason of course is that we live in a time where Hulse's critique is as fresh and relevant as when it was first written—maybe even more so. Authored with a kind and gracious tone, this work nevertheless attempts to tackle the insidious "easy-believism" of our day, and it is my opinion that he does so very effectively. While both accurate historically and nuanced theologically, the greatest strength of the work is actually his keen, biblical analysis of current evangelistic methods. Those methods are critically examined under the faithful searchlight of God's Word*—the only and ultimate standard of measure. *Hulse seeks to answer whether or not the fashionable trends of modern 'soul-winners' are articulating a right message and then whether they are utilizing a right methodology. He concludes that many are not, but he doesn't merely stop there. He also gives four historical examples of preachers from the 16th Century onward who didn't use the "invitation system," yet who were powerfully used by the Lord to win countless souls. If you are a preacher, evangelist, or Christian worker, this is the sort of book you need to read and heed. It might just revolutionize your approach to ministry. May our sovereign God give you the opportunity to do so.*

> — Lance Quinn is the pastor-teacher of *The Bible Church of Little Rock* in Little Rock, Arkansas and is also the Moderator *pro tem* of *FIRE* (The Fellowship of Independent Evangelicals).

Preface to the 2006 Audubon Press edition

Off the coast of Mozambique there is an island which is home to the Mwani tribe. The Bible has been translated into Mwani language. There was difficulty in the translation of Revelation 3:20, "Behold I stand at the door and knock". In Mwani culture a visitor does not knock at the door. He calls out for permission to enter. He waits for the invitation to come inside. Therefore the translators have translated the text, "Behold I stand at the door and call."

Whether the visitor knocks or calls, there must be an invitation to enter. The visitor may not force an entrance. Perhaps more than any other text of Scripture Revelation 3:20 highlights the fact that no person can be saved who does not embrace the Lord Jesus Christ by inviting him into the heart to be Lord and Saviour.

There are those who use Revelation 3:20 to endorse what amounts to a distorted view of God. They enshrine the free will of man as sovereign and use this text to assert that God cannot enter the human heart until given the right to do so by the sinner. In this way God is powerless to save sinners.

This can mean that no sinner can be saved because, "the hearts of men are by nature locked up and fast barred against Jesus Christ, their only Saviour."

How do we answer this? Psalm 110:1 declares, "Thy people will be willing in the day of thy power" (AV). Our omnipotent Father draws sinners (John 6:44). The Holy Spirit works in sinful hearts to turn them and in doing so he uses preaching and witnessing. The parameters of divine sovereignty and human responsibility are explored in this book.

To be converted is a matter of eternal importance. To come to Christ and to be united to him is to have eternal life. "He who has the Son has life; he who does not have the Son of God does not have life" (1 John 5:12). When united to Christ by faith the believer is justified and receives the gift of the person and work of the Holy Spirit. There is nothing more momentous for anyone than that! Deep concern that sinners should be saved has led to unbiblical methods to make it happen. The altar call is one such method, analysed in this book.

With regard to the altar call a good friend of mine who is a well-

known seminary professor, told me that as a child he went forward
every Lord's Day in response to the altar call. His Dad said to him
one day, "Son you do not have to go to the front every week!" This
draws attention to the nature of true conversion. You cannot be converted or be born again over and over again. When I was first converted I preached week by week in the open air in Pretoria, South
Africa. White people disdained listening at our open air services but
black people heard us gladly. I used to make an appeal for a public response. We then took enquirers back to the church to confirm their
decision to believe. One day a friend said, "Erroll have you noticed
that it is the same ones that make a decision every week?" That made
me think more carefully about my theology and about the method we
were using.

I recall visiting a mega-church in America of about 4,000 atten-
dees. I did not preach there but spoke to those who knew this church
well. I was told that the altar call method is used and that by this
method there is a steady flow of new members who come forward
week by week. No time is lost with those who respond to the appeal.
They are added to the church immediately. But the sad fact is that
church is static in growth. The back door is as big as the front door.
People are added easily and they leave easily. The method used is
shallow.

Once in a Southern Baptist church in America I concluded the
morning service in prayer. When I opened my eyes I was surrounded
by about twenty people all on their knees in the posture of prayer!
Each one was holding a card. The reason for this was that the pastor
instituted a means by which members of the congregation could move
forward at the end of the service, take a card with a specific prayer
request on it, and kneel and pray for a few minutes. The reason for
this practice was to conform with tradition which is employ the altar
call at the conclusion of services. In this instance those coming forward did not do so for salvation, for re-dedication or for healing. I am
not criticising my fellow pastor but cite this to show the kind of pressure that exists in some churches to maintain at least the appearance
of the altar call.

While in South Africa recently I was part of a congregation of a
Baptist Church. The pastor of this church is an expository preacher
with a fine biblical ministry but on this occasion there was a visiting
preacher. His sermon was lacking in depth and sadly was more about
himself than Christ. At the end of his sermon he made an altar call.

He invited those who needed to be saved to come forward. Nobody responded. He then made an appeal for those to come to front for consecration. Again no one moved. He then made an appeal for those who needed healing to come forward. An elderly couple went to the front. The overall impression given was that all this was artificial and fragmented prompted by the desire of the preacher to achieve a visible result.

In Great Britain there is a small number who strongly reject what they call the free offer of the gospel. They do this because they view sinners as total slaves and conclude that it is ridiculous to address them as though they possess spiritual power to repent and believe. They believe that God is dishonoured if he is made to appear powerless. Yet we cannot escape the fact that Christ does condescend to reason with sinners. That is why Revelation 3:20 begins with the expression "Behold!" It is remarkable that the omnipotent Christ should condescend to knock on the door of the sinner's heart. This book maintains the view that we are to freely offer Christ. These offers are to be made universally and without any inhibition whatsoever to all. The invitations of the Gospel are wonderful because they come from a glorious God. Preachers are to reason and to plead with sinners. The primary purpose of these chapters is to expound the biblical foundation for the invitations.

Erroll Hulse   2006

Preface to the 1986 Evangelical Press Edition

Writing this book has been like walking a tightrope across Niagara Falls. On the one side is the chasm of darkness, which results from a wrong view of God's sovereignty, and on the other are the raging torrents of error which follow shallow views of the state of man in sin. If reviewers are not themselves aware of the tensions that exist in the Bible then I am in for a hard time from them.

It is inevitable that readers will read first those sections of particular interest to them. For this reason, there is repetition. For instance, there is a full exposition of what is meant by preparationism in chapter 5, a brief outline of that subject in chapter 9, while Jonathan Edwards's view of the subject is described in chapter 10. It is important that each chapter stand on its own.

Chapter 5 is an important chapter because there the doctrinal foundations are laid. To make for easier assimilation I have broken that chapter up into six parts and rely on Andrew Fuller to provide some color at the beginning.

The Great Invitation of the gospel is an awesome and glorious subject. While we are in this world we should never cease making ourselves more proficient and winsome in the employment of the invitations.

The "appeal" is controversial. I pray that readers who do not agree with me may nevertheless be edified and enlightened when they learn why many great preachers have not used this method, and also that in our discussions we may exercise love and patience, which befit believers.

The subject of the "appeal" or "altar call" is more relevant in America than it is in the United Kingdom. I have been on ten preaching tours of various parts of the United States and Canada, but would not for one moment think that provides an adequate time to observe and discuss the different ways in which this system is used. To make up for lack of personal experience in the American scene I have sought the counsel of American pastors who have grown up in the orbit of the invitation system and who are thoroughly familiar with it. They have stressed the fact that the practice is mostly maintained because of tradition and culture. In addition to that there is the deep desire to counsel people and guide them to a decision for Christ. Also there is the persuasion that the method really works well and it is hard to think of any other. We often fail to attribute genuine results to the solid evangelistic and pastoral work that precedes the excitement of seeing someone go forward by way of visible response.

In this preface I would like to express my sympathy for those who may be shocked the "appeal" should be challenged. To reduce the sense of shock that some may feel, I would remind them that for well over 1800 years the Holy Spirit completed successfully all his work of saving sinners without this method. It was only with the advent of Charles Finney (1792-1875) that the "appeal" as an organized method really got underway. It was only on a limited scale at first because it was opposed by outstanding revivalist preachers like Asahel Nettleton.

It is important to stress at the outset that I regard a man like D.L. Moody as truly great. We do not allow differences of doctrine or method to distort our sense of proportion. In chapter 7, I discuss the danger of the "appeal" becoming an evangelical sacrament. Most evangelical preachers who employ the invitation system would be alarmed to think of the method becoming a sacrament, yet there are evidences that this is the trend. I am not accusing my brothers in the ministry of this. I know they are aware of the dangers, but I am earnestly pleading that we remember the lessons of church history. Today's erroneous practices, however well controlled now, become destructive heresies in the next generation.

Already in some quarters it is taught that those who come forward are thereby saved. For instance, Jack Hyles in his book Let's build an Evangelistic Church writes, "After the names are read and the people are lined up across the front, suggest that the membership come by after the benediction and shake hands with the new converts, encouraging them and welcoming them to the body of Christ. This too, can be a time of real blessing as the people share in the wonderful experience."

"In the benediction, the pastor could pray for the converts [italics his]. In other words, as the pastor leads the closing prayer he could say, "Dear Lord Jesus, bless Johnny who has been saved today. Help him to grow up to be a fine Christian man. Bless Mr. Jones who has been saved. We pray that he will be the kind of Christian You would want him to be. We're thankful that Mrs.

Johnson has been saved, and that Mr. Williams has found the Lord. We pray that You will bless Susie, Mary, Bill and the others and grant, dear Lord, that they will be great Christians." In other words, in closing have a prayer for God to bless the converts.1

The idea that raising a hand or going forward is equal to salvation or the new birth is found at grass roots level. For instance, a fellow elder who is a teacher in a secondary school said that a senior girl had put up her hand in response to an appeal in an evangelistic meeting. Unhappily there was a deep disappointment that no saving change whatever was evident in her life. Yet the minister involved insisted that if her hand went up that was infallible proof that she was saved. Some will argue that these are exceptional and extreme cases. My response is an appeal that we think the issue through and make sure our practices are based on Scripture and not on modern tradition.

Erroll Hulse   1986

1. Jack Hyles, Let's Build an Evangelistic Church, Sword of the Lord, 1962, p. 102.

1.
The title explained

The purpose of this book is twofold. The first objective is to show that there is no greater or more important invitation than that of the gospel. The Great Invitation of the gospel is anticipated in the Old Testament and fulfilled in the New. There should be no inhibitions in proclaiming the gospel of the good news of salvation in the person of Christ. There are no doctrines in the Bible which in any way limit the free offers and invitations of the gospel. The preacher of the gospel should never feel any inhibition in declaring the free justification held out by God to every sinner who will repent and believe in Christ.

In 1781 Andrew Fuller wrote a momentous book with the title, *The Gospel Worthy of all Acceptation*. His aim was to show that the gospel is fully compatible with the doctrines of grace. Indeed those truths strengthen the gospel and uphold its glory. Only when misunderstood do they hinder the freedom of gospel proclamation. My ambition is to be even more clear than Andrew Fuller, who was the great friend and supporter of that famous missionary pioneer, William Carey. I will demonstrate that the doctrines of God's sovereignty give preaching authority and the preacher unbounded confidence and enthusiasm.

The second part of this book is designed to show that there is no need to resort to methods which do not have the sanction of Scripture. The purpose of the earlier chapters is to demonstrate that everything needed for the preacher has been provided.

The preacher is free to exhort and command, to plead and implore, to reason and invite. He is an ambassador who speaks on behalf of the great King and whose purpose is to bring about reconciliation. Through preaching it is possible to appeal to people in the whole of their being — mind, affections, conscience and will. Various forms of inviting people forward to the front after services or after preaching have been devised. This method has become very popular. Many of those who use some form of public 'appeal' acknowledge that there are dangers. Church history shows over and over again that slight errors develop into serious errors which soon become heresy. In this case one of the most serious heresies of our generation has developed, namely, the idea that human decision is the cause of regeneration. This idea can predominate to the point where it becomes a sacrament, the meaning of which I explain in chapter 7.

When did the practice of calling people to the front begin? The history of the system is outlined in connection with the personalities who have devised, employed and refined the method. We will see from that just how prominent is the role of personality in this subject. Likewise chief exponents of the Great Invitation who did not use the altar call method are named and their reasons analysed.

In discussing the 'appeal' I have referred primarily to two books. The first is by R. Alan Streett and has the title *The Effective Invitation.*[1] This has the imprimatur of Billy Graham and is highly praised by W. A. Criswell of Dallas. It is comprehensive in its defence of the invitation system both from a biblical and from a historical perspective. The second book is a paperback by R. T. Kendall, which is a vigorous plea for calling people to the front with the title *Stand up and be Counted!*[2] As far as I know this is the first book of its kind in Britain which urges all ministers to use the 'appeal'.

How do we respond? This book sets out to examine whether the system has the sanction of Scripture. I am not aware of any other full treatment of the subject from this angle. A number of booklets have been written on the subject, but nothing which is comprehensive.

Defining the terms

It matters little whether we use the expression 'the appeal', 'the invitation system', 'the public pledge' or 'the altar call'. In essence all involve a call at the conclusion of meetings for people to come to the front to express their willingness to accept Christ, for salvation, to show rededication, to receive healing, or to give themselves to service, or for any other reason. The term 'altar call' is generally used to convey the idea of inviting people forward even if there is not a literal altar for them to come to.

We read of an 'altar' being erected 'unto the Lord in the forest,' in 1799. This was placed in front of the pulpit. Upon closer examination it appears that in fact the altar was a seat which some nicknamed 'the mourners' bench'. Mourners or penitents were invited to the altar if they were enquiring about the way of salvation. Their coming forward indicated that they were penitent.[3]

Later Charles Finney regularly used what was called 'the mourners' bench' or 'anxious bench' — a pew in the front of the church reserved for those coming forward, so that they might be counselled there, or alternatively taken into an enquiry room.

Different forms of the 'appeal' considered

The practice of calling for people to make a decision at the end of church services or evangelistic meetings is the policy of many evangelical churches. In most parts of America this practice is prevalent. It has been exported by American Christians to most other countries.

Since the North American missionary force is by far the largest in the world, we can readily appreciate the extent to which calling for public decisions has become a standard and accepted evangelistic form.

All kinds of formulas or methods have been devised to bring people to a decision. A typical approach is like this:
1. Personally acknowledge that you are a sinner.
2. Say that you believe in Christ's substitutionary work.

3. Decide to take your share of what Christ has done for
everybody.

4. Tell somebody today what you have done.

Many variations of this kind of procedure exist, but they
all have in common the matter of making a decision, either
by a prayer, or by signing a card, or by holding up a hand, or
by standing up to signify a response.

As we have seen, there is the concept of urging people
to come to kneel at the front of the congregation at an
altar rail. Of course, there is no significance in the altar
rail itself. It can be a penitent bench or it can be an area
in front of the church or perhaps a room at the back. This
method is unusual today. It is superior to other ways because
of its emphasis upon repentance.

Salvation is not the only reason for calling for decisions
or getting people to come forward. Backsliders can also
be called to come forward as a token of their repentance.
Those who are seeking a powerful experience of the Holy
Spirit, commonly called the 'baptism of the Spirit', may
also be invited forward. Again, in some churches those
who are looking for physical healing are invited to come
to the front of the church for the laying on of hands or
for prayer. Yet another reason for calling people forward
at the end of a service is for perfect sanctification, that is
to receive the power to be completely holy.

I remember as a young believer going forward to receive
this blessing. It was Guy Fawkes Night 1953 and we had
enjoyed a fiery sermon, far better than any firework dis-
plays. The preacher was Maynard James. It was convicting
preaching and the offer to provide perfect sanctification
seemed too good to be true. Subsequently I have sorted out
the difference between definitive or initial sanctification
in Christ and progressive sanctification. But I mention
this to show how calling people to the front is used for a
variety of reasons. At the end of a campaign the evangelist
usually tells how many came forward for various reasons
and often the success or otherwise of the meetings is based
upon these results.

As far as Britain is concerned, in most instances where
the 'appeal' is regularly employed, it is confined to use in
calling people forward for salvation, that is to come forward

to receive Christ. One of my close friends worked for a year in a town in England where there was only one evangelical church. She attended every Sunday. The preaching, although poor in doctrinal content, was evangelical and devotional in character. Every Sunday evening, without fail, the minister called for people to come to the front to record a decision for Christ. During that year, as far as she could see, not one person responded. In view of the fact that the same people attended the exercise seemed futile. Nevertheless this minister felt duty bound to employ this method. It would be interesting to find out what percentage of ministers in Britain regularly use the 'appeal'. It is small. More may use the method occasionally.

In many Southern Baptist Convention churches in the U.S.A. a fourfold call to come forward is used:
1. To receive Christ.
2. To move a church letter.
3. To rededicate one's life.
4. To surrender one's life to missionary service or full-time service.

To 'move a church letter' means to settle one's church membership. Many move from one area to another and delay settling their church membership which takes place by a letter of transfer.

Often there are two special campaigns or 'revivals' every year, when a visiting preacher comes for a series of meetings. For many, going forward at these meetings becomes a way of life. One pastor described to me that from the age of eleven to seventeen, he used to go forward twice a year, making a total of fourteen times. One year his dad, an experienced believer, remonstrated with him by saying that it was not strictly necessary to go forward. Because the invitation system does become a way of life for many, they find it very difficult to understand an outlook which rejects the system entirely.

It is more or less taken for granted that all evangelists use the invitation system of calling people forward at the end of their meetings. A few, like John Blanchard, do not use it. Not to employ the method seems inconceivable to many evangelists. The number who come forward for decisions, rededications or other reasons seems the only way of assessing the success of a campaign or crusade. Especially is the invitation system associated with famous evangelists like Billy Graham and Luis Palau. The number who come forward are recorded. They are called 'enquirers', but all too often the term 'enquirers' is changed by enthusiasts to 'converts'.

Since Billy Graham is the best known of the evangelists it will help at this stage to refer in general to the crusades he held in England. We will discuss the actual method he uses later.

It is generally agreed that the best Billy Graham Crusade in Britain was the one at Harringay in 1954. Tremendous preparation was made for this three-month crusade by hundreds of churches. The percentage of those who persevered, that is of the number who came forward, is believed to be better than for any subsequent campaign. A year later a week-long crusade was organized for Wembley Stadium. I can speak of that occasion as an eyewitness because my wife and I joined in whole-heartedly and without reservations of any kind. We worked as counsellors every evening. Of the twenty-six people we counselled not one came to anything. Ours was not an exceptional experience. Many testified that Wembley was just not the same as Harringay and different reasons are given. Billy Graham returned to London in 1966, this time at Earls Court. The standard was nothing like Harringay. A minister I know well had oversight over a number of churches. He said that after six months not one of those who went forward was still in attendance at the churches of which he had an intimate knowledge.

It is very difficult to assess what percentage of those who go forward do continue. There is no doubt about the fact that some are gloriously and lastingly converted. Those who chronicle the crusades describe outstanding instances, especially if they are well-known people. The argument is put forward that if only a small percentage are converted that endorses the method. However, that is what is called 'pragmatism', endorsing something merely because it works. The biblical approach is to ask whether it is right. As far as I know, nobody has ever sat down to assess the harmful results of using these methods or to analyse the hardening effects on those for whom it has not worked.

Also we have to come to terms with the truth that it does not always work. John Marshall of Hemel Hempstead tells of a widespread evangelistic campaign in his area of Hertfordshire in which the claim was made that 500 had been added to the churches. He carefully checked this claim with other ministers and discovered that no lasting additions had been made to the churches at all. There may have been a total of 500 raised hands or signed cards, but the commitment somehow evaporated.

R. T. Kendall has spoken of the visit of Billy Graham to Westminster Chapel for a Sunday evening service as a great event in the history of that church. Dr Graham rose from a sick-bed to fulfil the engagement. At the end of the service about eighty people went forward. I have always been positive about R. T. Kendall's enthusiasm for evangelism. I have always said to Kendall's critics, 'Better the evangelism he does than that which others never do.' I wholeheartedly agree with his work of going into the highways, streets and alleys of Buckingham Gate, and even getting into Buckingham Palace as well, if possible, to reach Her Majesty's staff and troops of the guard. I say this to remind my readers that we are devoted to evangelism 100 per cent in practice and in word and also to point out that R. T. Kendall would not let eighty new people slip through his fingers. But how many of those eighty new converts attend regularly? How many have been baptized? I am told that the result is good. One has definitely been baptized. I rejoice in that. It is excellent. But where are the other seventy-nine? Whatever the outcome, it should be clear that people moving to the front of a church after a service may look wonderful, but how much depth is there in it? This we must appraise fairly, honestly and realistically.

Before we examine the history of the invitation system and its usage today, it is essential that we establish the fact that the Scriptures provide an invitation to sinners which is perfect and which does not need addition. When some hear that we do not believe in using the 'appeal', they query whether we believe in urging sinners to be saved. They question whether we believe in a gospel which is unfettered and free. It is most important that it is proved beyond all doubt that we believe in the full and free overtures of the gospel to all sinners. It is because we believe this that we maintain that it is misguided and harmful to add methods that are not found in Scripture.

The issues involved demand careful and serious attention. The contents page will quickly reveal the scope of the subject. Some readers may already be convinced of the biblical nature of the freedom of the gospel and the extent to which it can be applied. They may wish therefore to proceed directly to the controversial chapters 6 to 11 and use the first chapters for reference purposes only. By all means do that if you wish, but I am persuaded that the urgency of the gospel is such that we should never assume that we know all about the way it should be presented.

If I were given the health and strength that Moses enjoyed and blessed with many years of consecutive ministry as a preacher, I would still at the end of that time be studying the Bible for the best ways of presenting the gospel to sinners and the best arguments to be used to bring them to repentance towards God and faith in our Lord Jesus Christ.

The method we will adopt is first to show that care is needed if we are to do justice to the foremost truths of the Bible. The gospel is simple, but it is also profound, as we will see in the next chapter. Secondly, we must come to grips with what is involved in inviting people to Christ. Since this subject is comprehensively anticipated by Isaiah the prophet, I have used Isaiah chapter 55 as a basis to explore the parameters of the Great Invitation of the gospel.

From there our next concern is to open up the foremost invitation texts of the New Testament. That will prepare the way for us to grapple with the doctrines related to the invitation.

Footnotes
1. R. Alan Streett, *The Effective Invitation*, Fleming H. Revell, U.S.A. 1984.
2. R. T. Kendall, *Stand up and be Counted*, Hodder and Stoughton, 1984.
3. As above, p. 52.

2.
Coming to Christ - simple yet profound

The method of grace presented by God in the Bible forms an enthralling subject. It amounts to this: all things are now ready, come to the feast! Who is to come? All are invited. Everybody is invited without discrimination. They are all invited to receive eternal life. But is it as easy as that? It is not! In one way it is very simple, but in another it is profound. The call to come to the waters of life is universal, but there are conditions. Those who come must come empty-handed. They are to come as penitents and bankrupts. They must come repenting and believing. That is where the whole matter becomes profound. To what extent must those who come repent and believe? Obviously, just an assent of the mind will mean little. The devils believe and tremble. Repentance means a real change of heart, without which there will be no lasting loyalty to Christ.

Our Lord said, 'I tell you the truth, unless you change and become like little children, you will never enter the kingdom of heaven' (Matt. 18:3). Coming to Christ like a little child and trusting in him for forgiveness and salvation is simple enough. But to gain a disposition to want to do such a thing, while it seems simple, involves an act on God's part. This act involves a new creation — in short, a miracle. At what point does God do his part and where do we do ours?

There could hardly be a more relevant subject because over-simplification of the gospel has become universal. It is very easy to make a little formula and imagine that an application of it can make people Christians. This can be done by thinking of God as mechanical, so that all that

happens is that God responds like a slot machine. You insert
the right coin and instantly out comes the desired result!

Coming to Christ would be a very simple matter if the
above concept were true, but it is not. It is false because
man's sinful disposition prevents him changing his own
heart. He is responsible to do so. 'Get a new heart', says
Ezekiel the prophet (Ezek. 18:31), but when it comes down
to it, the sinner cannot make himself a new heart because
of his love for sin and because of his enmity against God
(John 3:18; Rom. 8:7,8). Jesus said, 'No one can come to
me unless the Father who sent me draws him' (John 6:44).
So here we have to tread carefully: man is responsible; man
is unable. We must avoid falling into the trap of making a
false conclusion, namely, that man is not responsible because
of his inability. His inability is a moral one and therefore
he is responsible.

Each of the above truths — man's responsibility and
inability — can be fully proved by Scripture. Both must be
given full weight. The two must not be set up against each
other. Neither must be weakened or reduced because of
the other. It is not difficult to grasp that man's sinful nature
renders him unable to make himself a new heart. Anyone
who does not see this shows that he has not grappled
realistically with the unbelief of the ungodly. It is when
we reason with unbelievers on a personal basis that we come
to see that it is the hardest thing in the world to get a person
to have a new heart.

We should always do justice to both human responsibility
and inability. We must accept both because both are equally
in Scripture. We should always make sure that we allow the
two truths of human inability and human responsibility to
stand alongside each other without tampering with them.

For instance, we must never permit it to be said that
because the sinner is unable, he is not responsible. The
drug addict or alcoholic will often claim that he is not
responsible for his addiction because he cannot help himself. He says he is unable to help himself. We deny that.
All along the line the addict is fully responsible. God will
hold him accountable. Likewise the sinner could plead
that he cannot help hating and blaspheming God. He got
that God-hating nature from Adam. He was born with it.

Therefore he may plead that he is not responsible. We oppose that reasoning. The sinner may not reduce his responsibility by pleading his inability.

It is at this point that we have to reckon with the sovereignty of God. Because man has rendered himself impotent and because he is in a state of alienation towards God, it requires an act of divine, omnipotent power to change that sinner's heart and mind. As God is sovereign in creation, in providence and in the administration of this world's affairs, he is also sovereign in salvation. We only have to read the first chapter of Ephesians or the ninth chapter of Romans to see that. Even though we read about God's sovereignty in salvation we might be reluctant to accept it. Yet when we pray for sinners to be saved we always ask God to save them. We never ask for sinners to save themselves. Does God save sinners on purpose or by accident? Of course, he saves them according to his purpose. We cannot escape the fact of God's sovereignty in salvation. What we are afraid of is that a false conclusion should arise from this doctrine. Unhappily some have come to the erroneous conclusion that because God is sovereign, we need not assert man's responsibility. If God is all-powerful and sovereign he can do it all. Yet that is entirely wrong. If we say that in our hearts, then we are denying the truth of human responsibility. We simply must do justice to both truths.

For instance, we should oppose vehemently any suggestion that because God is sovereign in salvation the sinner can do nothing, that he is not responsible, that he can only wait for God to act and if God does not act he is lost anyway, because it is all a matter of God's sovereignty. Such thinking is entirely misguided. Likewise it is wholly misguided if Christians begin to reason within themselves that they can reduce their endeavour in evangelism because of the power and sovereignty of God.

We have to work at keeping the balance of truth. We are obliged to maintain both truths. If we neglect the biblical truths of the sovereignty of God and the responsibility of fallen men, we will soon be shallow and simplistic, as we saw at the beginning of this chapter. We will deceive people with our simplistic approach and not deal with the disease which was accurately described by Jeremiah when he said,

The heart is deceitful above all things
and beyond cure.
Who can understand it?

If there is the danger of denying the sovereignty of God,
there is the equal risk that we accept God's sovereign power
in an unbalanced way. We might fall into the trap of saying,
'Ah well, they can't repent, anyway! So what's the use of
our expending effort on evangelism?'

The answer to that error is to realize that God uses means
to achieve his purpose. Therefore anything less than whole-
hearted enthusiasm about evangelism is wrong. How can we
sustain our motivation and drive for evangelism? One way
is to observe the fulness and glory of the invitations of the
gospel. The Holy Spirit employs these as a means to draw
prodigals back home.

Before we go on to see that the invitations of the gospel
to all men are fully anticipated and described in Isaiah
chapter 55, it is important to stress that there are many
ways in which our zeal for evangelism is sustained.

We are always under marching orders to go because Christ
himself has commissioned his church to go and teach the
gospel to all nations (Matt. 28:18–20). This applies until
the end of time because our Lord says in that same commission, 'And surely I will be with you always, to the very
end of the age.'

There is also the motivation of compassion for men.
Usually this is the most powerful of incentives to employ
the means provided so that the lost will be saved. There are
several passages telling of the great judgement and of the
eternal punishment of the wicked. Matthew 25 and
Revelation 20:11–15 are two examples. The wonder and
glory of seeing people transformed by the gospel is yet
another motive to go out into the unbelieving world.

All that I will attempt in this book is designed to increase
our concern for taking the gospel to all peoples. There is
a grave dilemma for those who truly love evangelism and
who are committed to it 365 days a year and 366 days
every leap year. The dilemma is what to do when city-
wide efforts are put forward in which much harm is done
by over-simplification, and when there is even confusion

about what a Christian is. To stand aside is to risk misunderstanding. Yet many do stand aside, preferring to
concentrate on local church evangelism.

Whatever position the reader takes on these matters,
it is important to see that everything is provided in what
I call the 'Great Invitation'. Sometimes it is appropriate to
use the singular as it gathers up all the strands into one.
Nothing is lacking in the great gospel invitation. All we
need is there. We do not have to resort to our devices or
human inventions. If we fully and faithfully invite sinners
to come, the Holy Spirit will do his work. We have our
work and he has his work.

The inadequacy of theological vocabulary

We are indebted to J. I. Packer for his excellent little book
Evangelism and the Sovereignty of God. In this presentation
he discusses the tension that exists between what God does
as King and what he does as Judge.[1] Helpfully he draws
attention to the possibility of using the word 'antinomy'.
The Shorter Oxford Dictionary defines the word antinomy
as 'a contradiction between conclusions which seem equally
logical, reasonable and necessary'. Dr Packer points out that
we need to change the meaning of antinomy if it is to be
suitable for our purpose. We need to have a word which
means *'an appearance* of contradiction'. In spite of the
fact that antinomy literally means 'a contradiction between
conclusions which seem equally logical, reasonable and
necessary', J. I. Packer goes ahead and uses the word, having
explained that he is taking it to mean *'an appearance* of a
contradiction between conclusions'.

This subject of vocabulary and finding a word to help
us understand two of the greatest subjects of our Christian
faith — namely, the sovereignty of God and human responsibility — is very important. We must not be impatient.
When the apostle Paul was handling concepts immense and
glorious in their implications he compounded his own words
(for example, *sunarmologoumene*, 'fitly framed together',
Ephesians 2:21). Who today would be bold enough to
create a word to serve our needs? Personally I agree with

Dr Packer in his use of the word 'antinomy' even though it is not right in the precise sense. We are grappling with enormous concepts and many have been helped by having a word to express what would otherwise be hard to express.

Don Carson of the Trinity Evangelical Divinity School, Deerfield, Illinois, rejects the use of the word 'antinomy' in his book *Divine Sovereignty and Human Responsibility*[2]. He claims it is ambiguous and he opts for the word 'tension'. Technically Don Carson is correct. However, his opting for the word 'tension' is inadequate because the word is insufficient. Tension points only to the struggle and the pulling in opposite directions of the doctrines of divine sovereignty and human responsibility.

Is there such a tension? When we examine the frequency and degree with which this theme is presented in the Bible we must surely concede that it is a terrific problem. The tension is real and there does seem to be a major contradiction. For instance, Joseph's brothers came eventually to acknowledge their guilt for what they had done in selling Joseph into Egypt. They were fully responsible. However, Joseph assures them: 'So then, it was not you who sent me here, but God,' 'You intended to harm me, but God intended it for good to accomplish what is now being done, the saving of many lives' (Gen. 45:8; 50:20). Likewise we read in Acts 4:27,28 that while Herod and Pontius Pilate were responsible for their own wicked deeds, they did what God in his power and will had decided should happen beforehand. More difficult is the statement by Peter concerning the disobedient (1 Peter 2:8). They stumble because they persist in their stubbornness and rebellion. They are responsible for that, yet we read that God 'appointed' them (AV), or 'destined' them (NIV), to stumble at the Word.

By now someone may be thinking that all the discussion about antinomy could easily be resolved if I just used the better-known word 'paradox'. However 'paradox' is a word which often expresses opposite ideas with which we can easily come to terms. *Para*, 'alongside', points to the fact that we can have truths which do appear contrary or opposite at first, but when we look at them alongside each other there is no difficulty in understanding them at all. For instance, the apostle gives us several paradoxes in

2 Corinthians 6:8—10: 'Through glory and dishonour, bad report and good report; genuine, yet regarded as impostors; known, yet regarded as unknown; dying, and yet we live on; beaten, and yet not killed; sorrowful, yet always rejoicing; poor, yet making many rich; having nothing, and yet possessing everything.'

None of these is difficult to understand, but when we come to the sphere of human responsibility and divine sovereignty, we move into another league altogether. We have an example of these two truths being placed alongside each other in Matthew 11:27, 28, which we will be examining in detail later. That statement of our Lord tells us plainly that we depend upon his supreme sovereign power for personal salvation, and then we are immediately invited to come to him and respond to him personally by obeying his commands. Similarly in John 6:37 we are told, 'All that the Father gives me will come to me, and whoever comes to me I will never drive away.' The first sentence declares the sovereignty of God and the second affirms human responsibility.

How can these things be? The issue has taken up the greatest intellects and involved the foremost Christian writers in attempts to make simple what is most profound. How many believers truly hold to both divine sovereignty and human responsibility without confusion and without compromising one or the other? Because the subject is complex the word 'antinomy', in spite of its deficiencies, is helpful. Scientists use the word to describe light which consists of both particles and rays. Now a ray will never be a particle, and particles cannot be a ray. We are confronted with two different realms: particles and rays. Likewise with this subject of the gospel and its invitations we are confronted with the realms of God's grace, his will and his power to save whomever he will, for as Jonah discovered, 'Salvation comes from the Lord' (Jonah 2:9). As Jonah was powerless to get himself out alive, so sinners are powerless to save themselves, yet unquestionably they are responsible. As Peter puts it, 'Save yourselves from this corrupt generation' (Acts 2:40).

Whatever term we opt to use, antinomy or tension, the main issue is that we must accept God as King and Judge —

King to give salvation to whomever he pleases, and Judge to judge us for our responsibility. We are obliged to submit to this, accept it, believe it, act upon it and never fight against it or resent it.

With regard to the problem of terminology, we still need to find a word which expresses the tension that exists. Perhaps we should encourage those theologians who possess outstanding linguistic ability to compound a word in English, or borrow a suitable word from another language and anglicize it. No inhibition should be felt in attempting such a thing. We are dealing with divine subjects and should not be surprised to find that our vocabulary is inadequate. Languages are not static. They are organic. They are there to serve us, not we them.

Footnotes
1. J. I. Packer, *Evangelism and the Sovereignty of God*, p. 18 ff.
2. Don Carson, *Divine Sovereignty and Human Responsibility*, Marshall, Morgan and Scott, p. 257, note 38.

3.
The great invitation of Isaiah 55

It would be fair to say that Isaiah is *the* evangelical prophet of the Old Testament. An evangelical is concerned to spread the good news of salvation. To be an evangelical in today's context is to emphasize salvation by faith in the atoning death of Christ and to stress personal conversion. It includes faith in the infallible reliability of the Bible as God's Word written, faith in the resurrection of the body, the judgement to come, eternal heaven and eternal hell. An evangelical is especially concerned with the highest possible well-being of people, that is, their eternal salvation.

All the prophets were evangelical, but none more so than Isaiah. As far as doing the Ninevites good was concerned, Jonah was rebelliously evangelical. Elijah by contrast was passionately evangelical. So how can we say that Isaiah was *the* evangelical prophet? The answer lies in his proclamation of the coming of the Messiah. To Isaiah especially were revealed the sufferings and triumph of Christ, together with visions of the ultimate universal spread of his kingdom. Ezekiel was given more insights into the person and work of the Holy Spirit than most of the other prophets, while Jeremiah foretold precisely the terms and nature of the New Covenant. But it is Isaiah whose description is so detailed that you can almost see Christ being beaten with many blows, carrying the cross to Calvary and after that being buried in a tomb (Isa. 52:13--53:12). As soon as Isaiah's portrayal of the agonies of the Messiah is complete, there begins a glowing description of the widespread enlargement and spiritual prosperity that will follow. He likens the Messiah's cause to an enormous tent which has to be enlarged to its utmost capacity in order to accommodate the increase.

And how will all the peoples of the world be drawn in? Isaiah 55 provides the answer. It will be by the proclamation of the gospel. A wonderful result will be achieved by the invitations sent out on a universal scale.

Isaiah 55 anticipates all the principal terms and ingredients of gospel proclamation. These can be cross-checked with the New Testament. Every preacher is an ambassador for Christ (2 Cor. 5:20). Every herald of the gospel ought to check his message and his manner constantly to make sure that he acts according to the commands of his Sovereign. The King of kings has sent his ambassadors and it is imperative that they be diligent in every respect.

The gospel contains an unrivalled invitation for the following reasons:

1. It comes from the Creator of the universe.
2. It contains the good news of life for everyone.
3. It contains personal instructions as to what each individual must do.
4. It is presented in a manner which shows the sincerity of its author.
5. It offers great riches.

1. The invitation comes from the Creator of the universe

We all know what an invitation is — an invitation to a wedding or a banquet, or to dinner with friends or to a concert. When we analyse the nature of an invitation we soon see that the most important factor is the person who invites. If it is an illustrious person or prestigious personality, then we feel privileged and honoured. The second factor is the advantage of what is offered. There may be tremendous enjoyment and satisfaction involved. A third factor is our ability to fulfil any conditions of time or travel or expense in order to fulfil the terms of the invitation.

The parables of Jesus are unique in their power to illustrate the simple things of life. His parable about the king who prepared a great wedding banquet and sent out his invitations describes exactly the nature of an invitation

(Matt. 22:1–14). The foremost feature is that of the person who invites. The king was offended when his invitations were rejected and when his ambassadors were maltreated. The banquet was in keeping with the character of the majesty of the king. It was magnificent. There was no difficulty or inconvenience in attending the wedding. Everything was provided.

With these observations in mind we should admire the amazing love, kindness and condescension of the Creator of the universe in coming to those who have nothing, and deserve nothing, to offer reconciliation and the enjoyment of paradise, which was lost, but which will be restored. The forgiveness he offers is complete. He will freely pardon those who accept his invitation. To those who return to him he gives an abundant pardon.

The perfection of this pardon and the certainty of its duration are expressed in the offer of an agreement: 'I will make an everlasting covenant with you, my unfailing kindnesses promised to David' (Isa. 55:3). This covenant is prepared by the Father of our Lord Jesus Christ, who declares his willingness to bind himself to the one who accepts his invitation. As King David was loved, preserved and raised to be King of Israel, so David's God will affectionately embrace those who return to him for pardon. He will make them kings too. He will preserve and keep them always.

We see then that this invitation does not come from a national ruler or prime minister, or from an earthly monarch, but from our Creator. All earthly invitations are restricted to time and limited by the persons from whom they come. This invitation comes from the source of life and power.

Surely this reality of the transcendent glory of this person who is the fountain of all life must impress us, especially when we compare that glory with our own sinfulness, unworthiness, frailty and insignificance. That he is most ready to make an unbreakable covenant with us is staggering. What are the terms of this covenant? When we look into it we find that God binds us to himself and says, 'I will make an everlasting covenant with them: I will never stop doing good to them, and I will inspire them to fear me, so that they will never turn away from me' (Jer. 32:40). It is called the new covenant (Jer. 31:31–34; Heb. 8:8–12).

Included in the terms is this clause: 'I will forgive their wickedness and will remember their sins no more.' The ground upon which God does this is imputed righteousness. To impute means to put something upon a person. All that Christ did in his life and death on our behalf is reckoned to our account. Imputation is well illustrated when Joshua has his filthy clothes removed and pure, clean clothes placed upon him (Zech. 3). The filthy clothes represent our sins and it is because of Christ's death that our sins are blotted out, or, as the prophet Micah vividly states it, God hurls all our iniquities into the depths of the sea. God's justification of the believer is the first and greatest blessing he gives. A clear definition of justification reads as follows: 'Justification is an act of God's free grace, whereby he pardons all our sins, and accepts us as righteous in his sight, only for the righteousness of Christ imputed to us and received by faith alone.'

The completeness and finality of this provision should be stressed. It is the basis for everything else. The reason why it is not always possible to begin with this basic truth is that it is not regarded as relevant by the unbeliever until he recognizes his need. When a sinner has an encounter with God and is alarmed and awakened to the reality of his eternal lostness, then this truth about justification becomes music to his ears and joy to his heart. Then the righteousness of Christ is rich to him.

2. The invitation contains the good news of life for everyone

There is good news in the invitation of Isaiah 55. The news concerns living waters, which represent the very essence of life, joy and satisfaction that will never end. An invitation holding out so much should be closely examined. Is this invitation for some only, or is it for everyone? What does it say? 'Come, all you who are thirsty, come to the waters.' The Authorized Version expresses the invitation slightly differently and quaintly: 'Ho! Everyone who thirsts.' It is certainly a call to everyone. At the outset it seems that the invitation is confined or restricted only to those who are thirsty. Who are the thirsty? In reply to this question we see that the passage is speaking about the waters of life. There is nobody born into this world who does not desire life. Everyone earnestly wants life. Death is totally unnatural and hateful, ghastly and horrible to all mankind. We all hate death. We all search for life that will satisfy. The only time people want to die is when they experience prolonged physical or mental torture or are so old, tired or distressed that they long for release from suffering. Isaiah is stressing that everyone is included because he observes that they are all searching for life and show it by spending money, energy and time on the wrong things. They will never gain life that way. Note how eloquent and poetic Isaiah is:

> Why spend money on what is not bread,
>   and your labour on what does not satisfy?
> (Isa. 55:2)

Just look at how people devote themselves to living for money, for materialism, for worldly pleasure. But the satisfaction is short-lived. It is not spiritual. It never satisfies deep down. There is always a void, sometimes an aching void. Where God is not put first, marriages break down, families quarrel. And then death comes to overwhelm with sorrow because there is no foundation and no hope. The life offered here is grounded in the Creator, the source of life. That is why Jesus could say, 'I have come that they may have life, and have it to the full' (John 10:10). To be separated from the source of life is to forfeit life. No matter how hard we try to plan and live without God, we cannot escape the emptiness and meaninglessness that is there. Life without a purpose is like an ocean without a shore, or like space without a reference point. Think of the rich people of Hollywood and their parties. If fun and food are the purpose of life, why is it that there is so much unhappiness and frustration in Hollywood? People there and everywhere, whether rich or poor, struggle to find happiness and fulfilment. This unrivalled invitation is to all such, to all who long for life and satisfaction, especially to the great majority slaving away to create their own sources of satisfaction which cannot endure.

There is a New Testament equivalent to this invitation in

Isaiah. It is found in John 7:37,38, where we learn that
our Lord Jesus Christ stood up on the last and greatest day
of the Jewish Feast of Tabernacles and with a loud voice
made this call or invitation: 'If a man is thirsty, let him
come to me and drink. Whoever believes in me, as the Scripture has said, streams of living water will flow from within
him.'

Here again the extent of the invitation should be taken
from the promise held out. The life offered is the life of
God, irresistible, sparkling, flowing. None but those who
have actually come to Christ possess this life. Therefore
all the rest, that is all who do not have it, are addressed.
They do not have this water. They must therefore be thirsty.
Dehydrated people may be so ill that they are helpless.
Worldly people may be so regaled with the cordials of their
pleasures that they show no thirst. Nevertheless the invitation
applies in spite of that, for at any time they may become
aware that they are destitute of the living waters.

The universal application of these living waters to all
the world is expressed by the prophet Ezekiel (Ezek. 47).
He describes a river of life gushing out from under the
threshold of the temple. As it flowed it began as a trickle
but quickly became deeper and wider — ankle-deep, then
knee-deep, then up to the waist, then waters to swim in.
It flowed out into the world and wherever it went it created
fertility. Where it came to salty or brackish places it healed
them. Large numbers of fish multiplied in this water. This
water is the water of life, the water spoken of by the Lord
Jesus Christ. It is the river of life that has its source in Christ.
The life-giving stream has its source in his death and
resurrection. These waters flow increasingly as the church
grows, bringing life to souls throughout the world.

In anticipation of this source of life God calls on the
nations to forsake their idols:

> 'Turn to me and be saved,
>   all you ends of the earth;
>   for I am God, and there is no other'
>   (Isa. 45:22).

Similarly, in view of his Son's victory he says,

'Ask of me,
  and I will make the nations your inheritance,
  the ends of the earth your possession'
                                        (Ps. 2:8).

In distinction to the Jews, whose tribes are to be restored by Christ, he is to be a light to the Gentiles that God's salvation may be taken to the ends of the earth (Isa. 42:6).

To bring this about, the invitations of the gospel are to be sounded out. Every person is commanded to repent (Acts 17:30) and the gospel is addressed to all nations (Matt. 28:18—20). So that all may truly hear, the gospel preacher is to raise his voice in the public squares, at the head of the noisy streets, on the tops of walls and at the gateways of the city (Prov. 1:20, 21). With regard to repentance the preacher is not to discriminate when he is preaching. He is not to say, 'some of you', but, 'Repent and be baptized, *every one of you* in the name of Jesus Christ so that your sins may be forgiven. And you will receive the gift of the Holy Spirit' (Acts 2:38, 39).

Finally, we go back to Isaiah 55 and see that the invitation must be universal inasmuch as it calls on 'the wicked' to 'forsake his way and the evil man his thoughts'. Where in the world is there anybody who does not need to do just that?

3. The invitation contains personal instructions as to what we are to do

When we look closely at Isaiah 55 we see that the instructions are clear. What does it mean when twice it says, 'Come, buy!' Does that mean we must bring our cash? Not at all! The reference to buying is poetic. It simply means, 'Come and procure', or 'Come and obtain'. No stipulation about money is made. We do not have to bring anything, as the text says: 'without money and without cost' (v. 1).

The mistake made by most non-Christians is to think that they can bring something that will make them acceptable. We are invited to the wedding banquet, but we are not to come with our own wedding clothes (Matt. 22:1—14).

They are provided for us. This is a picture of the rejection of human merit. There is nothing at all that we can do to atone for our guilt and nothing at all that we can do to make us acceptable.

Having seen the negative, what not to do, what about the positive? What must we do in order to say 'yes' to this invitation? We must *listen.* The command is repeated: 'Listen' Why? Because by listening and obeying we will say 'yes', and in saying 'yes', receive eternal life. So what are the instructions? Here are the verbs all in the imperative: '*seek . . . call . . . forsake* [your] evil ways . . . *turn* to the Lord'.

To 'seek' is to search out the meaning and purpose of a matter. We are also to 'call'. This means to pray to God to ask him for our needs. A further instruction is to 'forsake evil ways'. To do this we need to recognize what they are and how vile they are, how offensive to God. We must then confess our guilt and turn our backs on those evil ways. This is not the meritorious cause of our salvation. The only cause and source of our salvation is Christ himself. Our forsaking of sin is an indispensable evidence that our faith in Christ is real and true. We cannot say we believe in him and at the same time wilfully go on in doing what he detests. Repentance is both initial and ongoing. It is initial in that it consists of a change of heart about God, self and sin. It is ongoing inasmuch as it continues to turn to God. True repentance results in life. The Jews rejoiced to hear that the Gentiles had been given a repentance unto life (Acts 11:18). With repentance we should seek to settle the issue of forgiveness of sin and justification because of the imputed righteousness of Christ. Following that and built upon it as an absolute necessity is what we call sanctification or holiness of life.

Is it right to tell a sinner to forsake sin before he has settled the question of saving faith, justification and salvation? Answer: sin is always abhorrent and must always be forsaken. Sin can never be excused. It often happens that sinners forsake all kinds of sinful practices before they become clear about justification. One of the chief sins they often forsake is indifference and carelessness about God. They do begin to listen. They attend to preaching regularly. They often quit blasphemy and evil talk. Often they begin to order their home lives properly. No improvements or repentances can be used as money or merit. But, judge for yourself, is it not always right to forsake all known sin? Of course it is right! However, the invitation to the sinner is to come immediately into covenant relationship with God, a relationship of forgiveness, of justification, and on that basis he is then constantly to resist sin and lead a life of holiness.

Does not the effort involved in forsaking sin and swimming to the lifeboat of salvation give cause for boasting? Can a person say, 'I swam and he didn't'? No! All that sinners do in drawing near to Christ before actually closing with Christ is due to the Father's grace. He draws sinners. He prepares them. He brings them. It is all of grace — before the event of conversion, at the event (being hauled into the lifeboat) and after (sanctification). By grace we are saved. The instructions include an urgent command to turn to the Lord. This means the sinner must actually come to Christ and embrace Christ as Saviour, Friend and Lord or Master. He must be reconciled to Christ and trust Christ.

When we stress that the sinner must forsake his evil ways and turn to the Lord, the objection can be made that all this involves quite a lot of activity. Also, it might be added that we are just complicating the simple gospel with conditions: 'Do this and do that!' After all, does the gospel not suggest that salvation can come in a look? If I just look at Christ sacrificed and believe in him I will be forgiven and justified in a stroke, in a flash, a moment! True, that is altogether true. Do it if you can. Yet in practice you soon discover that it is useless if people look and can see nothing because they know nothing about Christ and are ignorant. Faith must have definite knowledge to lay hold of and to trust.

That the sinner looks to Christ on the cross for forgiveness and salvation is always, and must always be, the central objective. At the same time there is a path or procedure to get sinners to do just that. Hence in Bunyan's *Pilgrim's Progress*, Pilgrim first forsook the City of Destruction and learned what the gospel was before he actually had the burden of sin fall off his back.

A knowledge of the truth is the normal prerequisite to salvation. As it is possible to err in over-simplifying salvation by saying to ignorant people that they can be saved by a look, so on the other hand we can err by over-stressing the amount of knowledge necessary to make faith viable. Also an excuse can be made by saying that I need a lot of knowledge first before I can close with Christ. Urgency is always there. *Now is the accepted time!* (2 Cor. 6:2). Yet I cannot believe something I am ignorant about. Here is one of the tensions we find in the gospel, as we discussed in chapter 2: I must know about Christ to come to him; I must not delay in coming to Christ. This matter is developed and discussed fully in chapter 5 under the section which deals with preparationism.

It is an awful danger to fall into the wicked excuse of saying, 'I am learning about Christ and therefore am not ready to come to him for salvation.' There are sadly those who are ever learning but never come to a saving knowledge of the truth. Secretly they cling to their sins still. There are others who know a lot, have a form of godliness, but it is only head knowledge. It is without power. It is dead and without the vitality of practical obedience and without love for other Christians. We are to reject and repudiate such people (2 Tim. 3:5). There are large numbers of them in some areas, but they never stay long in churches where demands are made of them according to New Testament standards. As soon as they see that self-sacrifice is required they disappear and either become wanderers or join a comfortable situation which demands little or no contribution.

True faith is not as easy as some make out. We must not substitute easy-believism for saving faith. To get saving faith often requires much seeking. When the sinner has it, it is a vital, living, pulsating thing which not only justifies but goes on to inspire a godly life.

4. The invitation is presented in a way which shows the sincerity of its author

The whole character of Isaiah 55 reflects earnest,

compassionate, loving and sincere concern. The substance and the way in which it is reasoned show concern and urgency. When so much is at stake it is of the utmost importance that the manner of the ambassador be in character with the King who sends him and the substance of the news he brings. It is good news and bad news. We have already observed the riches contained in the invitation. That is good news. The part that the hearers will think bad is that God's wrath is upon them in their present state. The fact that they are lost sinners will not please them. The ambassador must not be afraid or compromise that point. If he does, the whole object of reconciliation will be lost.

The ambassador must be earnest. His demeanour must be serious. His manner should be urgent and sincere. Since his invitation concerns eternal heaven or eternal hell, how could it be otherwise? His approach should be one of reasoning. The mind and heart have to be won. However, there can be no compromise with sin. This matter of reasoning about sin and forgiveness and about what is offered in the invitation must be patiently pursued. Here is an example of how it should be done. Say to the unbeliever: 'Why do you waste your money and your energy on that which does not satisfy? Why don't you come and enjoy delightful food? Why don't you submit to a worthy King and come to an agreement which cannot fail? Why don't you accept the challenge of a higher range of concept and thought which will liberate you from shallow and useless thinking?'

All this is the language of reasoning. You find it all the way through Isaiah 55. The invitation comes with words of authority that will answer all objections and deal with all excuses. The invitation comes clothed in substance and with promises which are reliable. When presented in its setting there is nothing empty about the gospel invitation. The invitation to the thirsty in Isaiah 55 comes within the framework of substantial, weighty reasons. The food offered is the best, the water nothing less than the living waters of eternal life. The covenant offered is one which is everlastingly secure. This is illustrated by the way its terms have already been faithfully met. It was made initially with David. To him was promised a descendant who would

take the throne and reign for ever (Ps. 89:1–4). This has
found fulfilment in King David's greater son, namely, Jesus
of Nazareth. He has become King over all kings. Around him
a new race is being gathered. Those who put their trust in
this leader will never be disappointed. The pre-existent,
uncreated, eternal and infinite second person of the Trinity
has taken manhood to himself. He has accomplished all
that is needful for us by his life, death and resurrection.
All power and authority in heaven and earth are now his.
How can you turn away from such a leader or be so foolish
as to trust in men who are mortal? What man can offer
forgiveness of sin? But here is the Lamb of God. He will
freely pardon. He will have mercy on all who turn to him.

The question of sin is an embarrassing one. Elsewhere
Isaiah reasons persuasively along two lines, firstly concerning the damning nature of all sin, and secondly that forgiveness is always possible even though the sin is extreme.

The prophet fearlessly exposes corruption, unfaithfulness,
religious humbug, hypocrisy in worship, murder, theft,
bribery, neglect of the fatherless and widows. He does this
all in the first chapter, where we also find the most eloquent
reasoning about forgiveness:

> 'Come now, let us reason together,'
>   says the Lord.
> 'Though your sins are like scarlet,
>   they shall be as white as snow;
> though they are red as crimson,
>   they shall be like wool'
>   (Isaiah 1:18).

Many, various and persuasive are the reasons which accompany the gospel invitation. An able ambassador will know
these reasons well and employ them appropriately at the
right time and suitably to the occasion.

For instance, there is the appeal to consider the past:

> 'Review the past for me,
>   let us argue the matter together'
>   (Isaiah 43:26).

When a life is wasted away on foolishness and emptiness, materialism and vanity, with no spiritual dimensions and no ultimate aim of purpose, then this should be pressed home. To waste one's life is a great evil. To live godlessly is the prime sin. Yet if in review of the past and in arguing out the matter there is acknowledgement of guilt and repentance, then the promise is there:

> 'I, even I, am he who blots out
> your transgressions, for my own sake,
> and remembers your sins no more'
> (Isaiah 43:25).

How reassuring is this promise of forgiveness! What more could the sinner want?

A major factor preventing non-Christians from embracing the gospel is fear of the repercussions. It is a great step to believe the gospel for forgiveness, but it can be an even greater move to trust Christ to deal with the repercussions: 'What will my friends and relations say?' 'How will my companions react?' Often those who are moved by the truth of the gospel are deeply troubled and fearful about the consequences for the future if they become practising Christians.

Our Lord never dealt with these difficulties by reducing the reality of the problem. Instead he stressed the importance of uncompromising discipleship: 'How can you believe if you accept praise from one another, yet make no effort to obtain the praise that comes from the only God?' (John 5:44). In a sustained appeal on another occasion he plainly described the division that would take place in families where some believed and some did not. The solution lies not in compromise, but in outright faith (Matt. 10:34–36). He is well able to supply his disciples' every need (Phil. 4:19).

The invitation to come to Christ in faith should mostly be presented in the form of reasoning and in a manner which is most tender, gentle and loving. But the same gospel can also be presented in the form of a command and be urged upon hearers with warnings of impending judgement. Not for one moment does this contradict the former love and tenderness, no more than the fact that loving parents can, for the well-being of their child, speak most threateningly to it.

The way in which Jonah preached at Nineveh can hardly be described as inviting. It was denunciation and pronouncement of impending doom. Yet indirectly his preaching acted as an invitation to repentance. Through the grace of God Jonah was highly successful.

The invitation can be accompanied with promises of reconciliation, joy and peace, or it can come clothed in the military uniform of sternness accompanied by the thunders of the law, judgement and the certainty of eternal hell for the impenitent. It is a major mistake to set up one form of presentation against another. Both sweetness and sternness are appropriate, depending on which aspect of the gospel truth is being preached.

The question is sometimes asked whether humour should ever be used in presenting the gospel. Spurgeon possessed a spontaneous humour and admits that he often found it necessary to suppress it. In one of his sermons he tells of some students who, having been saved themselves, were determined to rescue an unbelieving friend. They persuaded him to hear the best preachers, but he still did not believe. Last of all, they chose a preacher who sometimes made his hearers laugh. They took their friend and to their dismay the congregation laughed when he described a butcher who led his pigs into the slaughterhouse by dropping peas along the path. He then likened that to Satan, the slaughterer of souls, who takes men into hell by dropping peas for worldlings on the way to the slaughter. This convicted the unbelieving student and paved the way for his conversion. An instance like this does not prove the point that using humour is correct, but I would maintain that we must be human in our presentation of the gospel. By 'human' I mean that we should view our fellow men in their wholeness. We can reason, we can plead, we can appeal to their understanding and, as cited above, we can, if necessary, appeal to that part of their judgement which can see that it is ludicrous for humans to behave like pigs.

5. The invitation offers great riches

Isaiah promises the 'richest of fare' to those who respond to the invitation. It is only really in the New Testament that we can see fully what this means. Christ himself is the source of all the riches offered in the gospel. In his Godhood Christ is omnipotent, all-present, all-sufficient, inexhaustible, soul-satisfying and never failing. Only God could assert what he said of himself in the great 'I am' declarations, such as, 'I am the bread of life. He who comes to me will never go thirsty' (John 6:35), and 'I am the resurrection and the life. He who believes in me will live, even though he dies; and whoever lives and believes in me will never die' (John 11:25).

Instead of the frustration of wasting time and effort on schemes which will never satisfy, we are invited to have our souls delighted with the richest of fare (Isa. 55:2).

As we saw, the invitation itself comes from the Creator of the universe, whose gift to us is Jesus Christ, his Son. He is this rich fare because in his person and work every provision is made for us. When the gospel says that those who believe in Christ have eternal life, that refers to the quality of life enjoyed as well as its duration. It is divine life. It is the life received from Christ in union with him. Because it is the life of God there is no death in it. It cannot be destroyed. When man was first created there was the potential that he could live for ever and be provided with a guarantee that he would do so. He was given one condition: he had to be faithful. This one condition he broke completely. In doing so he died.

When through union with Christ life is restored, it is restored in such a way that the roadway to death is blocked up. When we accept this unrivalled invitation to embrace Christ and be joined to him spiritually two things happen. Firstly the Father accounts us as just in his sight. He justifies us on account of our union with Christ by faith. This has already been stressed, so we go on to observe the second provision, which is that union with Christ means that we have a new nature.

To have a new nature, a renewed heart and mind, is to be born again. It is to have a transformation of our affections, our minds and our wills. This work of new creation will be perfected in such a way that we will be secured from the possibility of sin. This is called 'impeccability'. It is a state in which we cannot sin. Christ's disciples have certainly not reached it yet, but they will. When they die their spirits are perfected (Heb. 12:23). On the resurrection day their perfect spirits will be joined to perfect, glorified, imperishable bodies (1 Cor. 15:35–54).

The riches of the next world
This life is incomparably rich because it is a life of knowing and enjoying God for ever. It is a life of exploring, appreciating and enjoying a new and better creation in partnership with God. This is rich indeed.

What will heaven be like? Peter calls it an inheritance that can never perish, spoil or fade (1 Peter 1:4). This inheritance is described by Christ as a place that he is preparing. He says that in his Father's house are many rooms. The Authorized Version says, 'many mansions'. The idea is of permanent residences, dwelling-places, spacious apartments. The picture is of a city in which a variety of homes are found. It will be a city of enormous size, a city called the New Jerusalem. This will be necessary because we will have perfect bodies with properties and qualities much better than those we have now. Our faculties of sight and hearing will be perfect. Our minds and affections too will be freed from all the destructive powers of sin.

A common mistake in this world is to place a higher value on personal possessions than on people. Heaven will primarily be an enjoyment of Christ and his people. This does not mean to say that there will not be a material creation to observe and enjoy (Isa. 65:17–25; 2 Peter 3:13). The new creation will be better than the present one, which has many places of interest and beauty. The new creation will be richer, fuller and more glorious by far, because it will be free from the appalling forces of evil which torture our present creation. We will have freedom to go in and out of the city, going out to explore and admire the wonders of the new earth and returning to share together.

Whereas now there are desperate struggles to possess a small piece of this world, the world of glory will be shared by, and be accessible at all times to all her inhabitants. We will enjoy it freely. We will not fight and war over it. We will enjoy all the new creation intensely because at all times we will delight in it in partnership and in perfect harmony with our Creator. What a contrast with the present scene, in which men blaspheme God and destroy his creation! All that is noble and glorious will be restored (Rom. 8:18–23).

Perhaps now we can appreciate better what is meant when Isaiah says that if we accept this unrivalled invitation we will delight ourselves in the richest of fare. There are endless riches in the Lamb of God to whom all sinners are warmly invited to come.

4.
The foremost invitations expounded

Having explored the fulness of the provisions and instructions of the Great Invitation of the gospel contained in Isaiah 55, we move now to the New Testament. From promise we turn to fulfilment. In doing so we soon discover that the promise was not greater than the fulfilment. In every respect the invitations made by Christ and his apostles are equal in substance and glory to those expressed by Isaiah.

We will concentrate on the most striking calls or invitations and discuss them in general before we examine three of the best known in detail. The three (Matthew 11: 27, 28; Revelation 3:20; 22:17) are chosen because taken together they embrace the main principles of our subject.

Remembering the principal features explained in the previous chapter, we may ask, 'What are the most striking invitations of the New Testament?' One which stands right out is the one Christ made at Jerusalem on the occasion of the Feast of Tabernacles. It was the last and greatest day of the Feast. The text says, 'Jesus stood,' which implies that he placed himself in a prominent position. It then says that he said with a loud voice: 'If a man is thirsty, let him come to me and drink. Whoever believes in me, as the Scripture has said, streams of living water will flow from within him' (John 7:37). Here we have the source of all the gospel invitations: 'Let him come to *me*.' Christ himself is the source of life. We notice too the prominence of faith: 'Whoever *believes* in me!'

The invitation is qualified. It says, '*If* a man is thirsty.' Obviously those who are not thirsty will not come. I have sought to deal with this from Isaiah 55 where similarly

38

Isaiah's call is to the thirsty. When we come to chapter 5 we will see that it is wrong to establish a condition and say that a sinner does not have a right to believe on Christ until he is thirsty. However, it should be obvious that those who are thirsty for real life are having their attention arrested by the terms of the invitation and also by what is promised, namely, 'streams of living water from within'.

The text implies unrivalled authority in the one who gives it. He is the Creator of life. He must be if he is able to cause living waters to flow from within those who believe. This brings us to an outstanding characteristic of these invitations and that is that they are solidly based on Christ's supreme authority and come within the context of deep and rich teaching.

This is well illustrated from the most frequently quoted invitation, namely, Matthew 11:27, 28: 'Come to me, all you who are weary and burdened, and I will give you rest.' I will explain this particular text presently, but in the meantime observe that although verse 27 forms part of the invitation, it is very seldom quoted. Verse 27 reads, 'All things have been committed to me by my Father. No one knows the Son except the Father, and no one knows the Father except the Son and those to whom the Son chooses to reveal him.'

Here we have an outstanding example of divine sovereignty being placed alongside human responsibility, as implied in the invitation, 'Come to me . . .' which follows. The same principle is used when our Lord declares, 'All that the Father gives me will come to me, and whoever comes to me I will never drive away' (John 6:37). On the one hand we have an assurance of God's absolute sovereignty, and on the other the comfort of knowing that anyone who comes will not be cast out or driven away.

A similar example in which great truth is joined to a fervent invitation is 2 Corinthians 5:20, 21: (20). 'We are therefore Christ's ambassadors, as though God were making his appeal through us — we implore you on Christ's behalf: Be reconciled to God. (21). God made him who had no sin to be sin for us, so that in him we might become the righteousness of God.' The textual numbers have been included in the quotation to highlight verse 21 which I regard as the most profound verse in Scripture. Here full reasons as to why the alienated should be reconciled to God are compacted into one sentence.

This passage and the others remind us that the invitations should not be separated from doctrinal preaching. Today it is common for appeals to be made at concerts or at the end of services which have consisted mostly of items of entertainment. The use of the word 'implore' by Paul is noteworthy. It is expressive of a whole-hearted, uninhibited appeal. The strongest, clearest reason follows to strengthen that appeal.

As we refer to the contexts of the gospel invitations in the New Testament we must surely be impressed by the fact that the divine nature of Christ, his power and his supremacy are joined to his invitations. These are joined to human need and the call to come to Christ in repentance and faith.

We will turn now in detail to three invitation texts to show that we should never feel any inhibition whatsoever as we make gospel invitations. These are full, free and sufficient in and of themselves. We do not need to go beyond them because coming to Christ is not a physical thing using hands or feet. As Paul says in Romans 10, we do not have to go up to heaven or go down into deep places. We do not have to travel abroad or even go up an aisle, because the Word is in our hearts (Rom. 10:6, 7). It is the Word that the Holy Spirit uses to persuade men.

Christ's compassionate invitation to the weary (Matthew 11:27, 28)

This passage has already been quoted. Upon the foundation of verse 27 the famous invitation of verse 28 is made. Three truths are established by Christ in verse 27 as follows:
1. The relationship between the Father and the Son is unique;
2. All affairs have been committed to the Son;
3. The Son sovereignly chooses to reveal himself to some sinners.

From the first two points we are reminded that we ought always to think of God as triune. Everything in creation and everything which occurs in God's providence is by concurrence. God the Father is the prime mover or cause. He works through Christ and by the Holy Spirit. In salvation the Father calls the sinner, Christ reveals himself to that same sinner and the Holy Spirit regenerates that sinner. If we always bear this in mind we can better understand the conversions reported in the New Testament.

For instance, have you ever wondered why it was that Jesus stopped under a sycamore-fig tree in the streets of Jericho, looked up into the eyes of Zacchaeus, the chief tax-collector of that area and called him by his name? There was a great crowd of curious people so that it was impossible to get near. For a short man like Zacchaeus there was no alternative but to take the undignified route up into the tree. Imagine yourself to be a famous preacher surrounded by hundreds of people and making your way along a tree-lined street. How could you know the names of the people? Would you think of stopping to locate a person above you in a tree? Sycamore fig trees have many leaves, so probably Zacchaeus was well camouflaged. How could you know the name and domestic details of the person you were talking to? Without supernatural knowledge or omniscience how could you know that there would be enough room and adequate food supplies for all your companions? How could you know whether the man would be willing to give large-scale hospitality? More important than all these details is the factor of personal salvation. That very day Zacchaeus was saved. Jesus said, 'Today salvation has come to this house, because this man, too, is a son of Abraham. For the Son of Man came to seek and to save what was lost' (Luke 19:9, 10). Here in Zacchaeus we have an example of Jesus revealing himself to a lost sinner. Zacchaeus' response was clear and enthusiastic.

Another outstanding instance of Jesus revealing himself to a stranger is recorded in Mark 2. You may remember that four men broke open a roof and lowered their paralysed friend into the crowded room in front of Jesus. Before healing the crippled man, Jesus startled all present with the words: 'Son, your sins are forgiven.' In other words, Jesus forthrightly announced his intention to save this man who up to this point was quite ignorant. Yet he received the

gift of a healed body and a redeemed soul all in the space of
a few moments. The instant, supernatural, powerful and
perfect healing of this hopeless cripple, who had to be
carried by four men, indicated to everyone present that
Jesus was almighty. If he commanded a miracle to be done
it was instantly accomplished. The striking feature, both
for those present and for us, is that the man's sins were
first forgiven without his saying anything or making any
request.

In the two cases cited we observe the sovereignty of Christ
in calling individuals to himself. His call is personal and it
is accompanied by the Holy Spirit's irresistible work within
those called. The absolute sovereign power of Christ to call
individuals is illustrated even more amazingly in the case
of Saul of Tarsus. The story is well known. Saul was bristling
with opposition to Christ and his church. He had dedicated
himself to full-time persecution, yet right in the middle of
these detestable activities Christ revealed himself to Saul
as personal Saviour. Nobody could dispute the nature of this
revelation of Christ. As God he willed to call Saul at that
time and in that manner. It was a mighty act of grace to
forgive his sins. To that mercy he added the gracious privilege
of service.

Now there is no way that we can choose an individual
and give commands to him as Christ did to Zacchaeus. There
is no way that we can pick an individual out of a crowd
and pronounce his sins forgiven. And certainly there is no
way that we could shine out of heaven with a light above
that of the sun and call a Jewish rebel determined to destroy
the church.

What we can do, and what we must do, is to extend the
invitation of Matthew 11:28 to all. If that invitation is to
be full of authority and substance, then we must reckon
on describing the sovereign divine Lord, for it is to him
that men must come for forgiveness and eternal life. Exposition of the attributes of God is an important and integral
part of gospel preaching.

We come now to verse 28 which, for the sake of clarity,
can be set out like this:
1. *Those invited* — 'all you who are weary and burdened'.
2. *The promise assured* — 'I will give you rest.'

3. *The direction given* — a. 'Come to me.'
   b. 'Take my yoke upon you and learn from me.'
4. *The encouragement provided* — a. 'I am gentle and humble in heart.' b. 'My yoke is easy and my burden is light.'

1. Those invited — 'all you who are weary and burdened'
Those who have to travel a long way grow weary. The word employed in our text is the same as we have in John 4:6, which describes the weariness of Jesus after his long journey. The word may be used to describe bodily or mental labour. The key to understanding the thrust here is found in Ecclesiastes: 'What does a man get for all the toil and anxious striving with which he labours under the sun? All his days his work is pain and grief; even at night his mind does not rest. This too is meaningless' (Eccles. 2:22, 23). What is life without God? All of it is meaningless, a chasing after the wind. No matter what we may turn to, if purpose is absent, if eternity is omitted, if our Creator is ignored, then all is utter vanity. Learning, pleasures, riches, fame, every project, every possession are all meaningless. Relationships with others may be rich and precious, but without assurance of their enduring into the next world those relationships all terminate at gravesides.

The weary then are to be found everywhere. Not far under the surface there is disillusionment, fatigue, disappointment and fear. To all who are thus wearied, to all who see the emptiness, the drudgery, the meaninglessness he calls, 'Come! My life is for you!'

The description 'burdened' refers to those who are weighed down, who find their toil too demanding. Men will bear heavy responsibilities and exert themselves tremendously for high rewards, but if those rewards turn from gold into clay how futile is the toil expended! Consider what a high proportion of the human race have to toil without high rewards. Many can scarcely eke out an existence. Especially is the call of the gospel to those who are not only troubled by the futility of it all, but burdened with poverty, exhaustion or sickness.

This invitation is a tender one. It is full of sympathy. Why are some born blind, deaf, maimed or crippled? We know that these things happen within the sovereign purpose

of God, and we also know that the invitation is especially
to such who may be doubly wearied and burdened by their
impediments or handicaps.

2. The promise assured — 'I will give you rest'
There is finality in the way this is expressed. 'Having come
to me, you will have been given rest and will continue in
that rest.' This is the rest of those who trust in the Lord.
They are like Mount Zion which cannot be shaken, but
endures for ever (Ps. 125:1). Those who are justified by
faith have peace with God (Rom. 5:1). This rest is the
settled rest of salvation. The fruit or outcome of it experi-
mentally is peace of mind (Isa. 26:3; Phil. 4:7). The world
does not know this rest, or the peace that results from it,
because it is something created and sustained by God
(John 14:27).

The power of this invitation lies in the 'I' which expresses
the authority of Christ. Only he can say, '*I* will . . .' The
previous verse is one of the clearest statements in Scripture
concerning the Godhood of Christ. He is well able to give
this rest.

*3. The direction given — 'Come to me, Take my yoke upon
   you and learn from me'*
Note that this is not coming to Christ only as a once-off
encounter. It is coming to Christ and becoming one of his
disciples or learners. The pupil must take on the responsibility of learning about Christ. He must learn the commandments of Christ and obey them. 'This is love for God: to
obey his commands. And his commands are not burden-
some' (1 John 5:3).

A yoke or wooden frame is used to spread the load and
make it lighter. It is absolutely certain that discipleship
involves responsibility. Some may say that they have enough
problems without adding more, yet in a strange way the
addition of this weight reduces all the others. Christ's yoke
sweetens and lessens all the other burdens of life.

*4. The encouragement provided — 'I am gentle and humble in
   heart . . . my yoke is easy and my burden is light'*
The first statement is foundational to the second. The

character of Christ is such that he is all kindness to those who are joined to him. He loves them dearly. He is gentle and humble in heart. He is the true Shepherd who cares for his sheep. The law of God is an intolerable burden to those at enmity with God (Rom. 8:7,8), but those who are being conformed to Christ find his requirements are spiritual, holy, righteous and good. His way can sometimes be difficult because of this present evil world, but Christ is with his people always to help them. If the believer has to pass through fire or flood he will not be engulfed or burned (Isa. 43:2).

Christ knocking at the door of sinners' hearts (Revelation 3:20)

Since there is disagreement over the meaning of this text it is important that we look at it carefully. On the one hand there are those who use it to portray fallen sinful man as a sovereign lord of his own heart, who will only open his heart if he feels like it, while Christ is portrayed as weak, defeated and dejected, standing out in the cold and the rain. So horrible is this representation that some over-react and deny that the individual is being addressed at all. They maintain that it is a church that is addressed, not an individual. However, both groups are wrong. For those who use the text to depict Christ as weak and dependent on the sinner's will are in error. Those who say the invitation is to a church only are also wrong, for the text says, 'If *anyone* hears my voice,' not, 'If *the church* hears my voice'.

We do well to look at the verse more closely: 'Here I am: I stand at the door and knock. If anyone hears my voice and opens the door, I will go in and eat with him, and he with me.'

The dreadful state of those addressed
The last of the seven churches addressed by our Lord is the one at Laodicea. The church there was in an extremely bad spiritual state. The Laodiceans are described as lukewarm — neither hot nor cold: 'You say, "I am rich; have acquired wealth and do not need a thing." But you do not

realize that you are wretched, pitiful, poor, blind and naked.'
These are strong terms telling of a deplorable condition.
The words 'wretched and pitiful' tell of an abject condition,
while the three terms 'poor, blind and naked' suggest that
the majority of these people were not converted. To remedy
their poverty they are counselled to get a living faith. Peter
gives the picture of faith being tested like gold in refining
fires (1 Peter 1:7). Our Lord says here that a living faith is
tried in the fires of testing like gold. The Laodiceans did
not possess this living faith. Moreover they are described
as blind. In other words, they had no spiritual discernment.
They were like those who Jesus said needed to be born
again so that they could *see* the kingdom of God. Most
devastating of all is the charge that they were naked. Their
nakedness is described as 'shameful'. The white clothes
that must be obtained represent imputed righteousness
(Zech. 3:1—5). The wedding garment is an essential without
which a person is rejected (Matt. 22:11—14). It is clear
that many of the Laodiceans stood in need of the white
clothes of salvation.

What, we may ask, was happening at Laodicea? Unconverted people do not usually predominate in a church —
or do they? History shows that all kinds of people can
congregate in churches and that sometimes large proportions
of interested, half-committed, unconverted people are
regularly present. Sometimes it is said that it is futile asking
people to *come* to church. Rather we are to *go* to people
where they are. That is correct, of course, but only if we
remember that we are to do all we can to persuade those
outside to come inside. This is because God's way is to
save people under the preaching of the Word and in the
company of his people. When we examine history carefully
we discover that it is rare for people to be saved in isolation.
It would seem that the majority have been brought to
salvation in churches, that is under, through and by the
instrumentality of preaching.

We are not to imagine that the assembly at Laodicea
was not mixed in character. The New Testament shows
that a regenerate church membership based upon what
we call 'credible professions of faith' should always be
the aim. Doubtless the Laodiceans had done this, except

now the professions were not very credible or convincing. Our Lord, who sees into the hearts, knew that these Laodiceans were in a desperate state. They were weighed in his balances and found wanting. Hence the alarm in his urgent warning and his command to them to repent.

The opening of the heart to Christ is the great design of the gospel

The AV rendering, 'Behold! I stand at the door,' is more expressive than the NIV, which reads, 'Here I am! I stand at the door.' 'Behold!' is a striking way to draw attention to the wonder of the matter. He who created the universe and has all power in his hands condescends and humbles himself to stand outside a vile sinner's heart. That is a just cause of amazement. We should wonder at it. We should behold it. What is this, that God should stoop to so low a threshold and engage in knocking, standing and waiting? Why does he do it? The answer is that the opening of the heart of fallen man to God is an object of immense value. The angels of God rejoice over one sinner that repents. The inhabitants of Mount Zion, the city of the living God, exult in it and are moved by it.

When a sinner's heart is opened something has taken place which is very hard. The door of the heart is bolted and barred. Remember the prejudice of Saul of Tarsus. He was implacably opposed to Christ and would have the door of his heart shut to Christ as firmly as the great doors which guard the bullion of the Bank of England. Yet that door swung open and he said, 'Lord, what will you have me to do?' Of such moment is this matter of bringing the sinner to open the door that I have devoted to it the chapter on the new birth, for nobody will ever open up until he is changed within. The power of God making a sinner willing precedes the sinner opening the door of his heart (Ps. 110:3 AV).

It is not true that it is easy to believe. To persuade people so to believe in Christ that they give their lives to him is hard. That God should be manifest in the flesh is the supreme wonder of all ages. That sinners should believe on him is a marvel associated with that wonder, as we see in 1 Timothy 3:16. Beyond all question the mystery of godliness is great:

He appeared in a body,
  was vindicated by the Spirit,
was seen by angels,
  was preached among the nations,
was believed on in the world,
  was taken up in glory.

Every time a transgressor exercises saving faith in Christ
the trumpets of joy sound in heaven. No matter how dismal
the background, no matter how dire the deeds, the one who
before was heading for destruction now becomes a treasure
of heaven, a jewel to be set in the crown of Christ. We can
see why it is that Christ condescends not only to come and
knock, but to stand, to wait and continue knocking.

What it is to open the door to Christ
The concept of opening the door to allow Christ's entrance
conveys the truth of willingness to receive him to the point
of action. God's action is regeneration. Man's action is conversion. In most instances conversion in Scripture describes
the manward side: what man experiences when he turns to
God. No person can be saved unless he himself turns. This
turning or converting is to leave the realm of self-trust to
trust oneself to another. We know that the quickening work
of the Holy Spirit always precedes conversion, but concern
about safeguarding the Godward aspect should not prevent
us from exploring and describing what people actually
experience in conversion. The reason why unbelievers lock
and bar Christ out is that they want to run their own lives.
To come to the actual point of surrender, of going to the
door and opening it, is the most important and tremendous
decision a person ever makes. Just how does a person open
the door of his heart to Christ? He opens by prayer, by
saying, 'Lord I open my life to you, come in.' He says in
effect, 'I now abandon my resistance, I now quit my
opposition, I welcome you to rule my heart.'
To get up and actively open the door involves a conscious
effort of the will. The will does not operate on its own. It
is moved by the understanding and affections. A life-changing
step is not brought about lightly. Such a step is made only
when the objections and excuses of the understanding have

been removed and the disaffection and disablement of the heart have been overcome. That is the reason why it is harmful to induce people to open the door by sheer emotion. If their minds and hearts are bypassed it means that there will be no change. To illustrate this, take the drunkard. When the inveterate drunkard is in trouble he will repent most easily and will assure you that all his resolutions to reform are sincere. He will promise that if you give him money he will use it for food and clothing. But no sooner does he disappear round the corner but he is overcome again by his raging desire. His feet take him directly back to his alcohol.

What it means for Christ to knock at the door
The knocking of Christ is the preaching of the gospel, with its reasonings, its entreaties, its commands, its beseechings and implorings, its warnings, its offers and invitations. All this is so that the lost soul should close with Christ and be saved. Powerful gospel preaching is the clearest way in which Christ knocks to enter the soul.

Christ also knocks at the door of the soul by the voice of conscience. Every person is born with a witness in himself which tells him what is right and what is wrong. The conscience responds to gospel truth and says, 'That is right! You are a sinner, you need to be saved, you ought to say "yes", you ought to believe in and receive this Redeemer.' The conscience bears witness to the truth, whether it comes through a preacher, a friend in conversation, a tract or book, or the Bible itself. The conscience bears witness to the rightness, the importance and the necessity of obedience. The conscience testifies and says, 'If your neighbour can be a practising Christian, then you can be too.'

The knocking of Christ at the hearts of sinners includes acts of providence, such as provisions and benefits which magnify God's love and his affording of opportunities to repent (Rom. 2:4). Providence also includes affliction and sorrows, whereby the unrepentant are warned of the brevity of life and the importance of preparing to meet God at the judgement. Times of sickness, loss or disappointment are especially designed to lead to thoughts about eternity.

The fact that Christ stands to knock indicates his

long-suffering and patience. 'O Jerusalem . . . how often
I have longed to gather your children together, as a hen
gathers her chicks under her wings, but you were not willing!'
(Matt. 23:37.) How often! He laboured hard among them.
As he did so their responsibility increased. All day long he
knocked, as it says in Romans 10:21: 'All day long I have
held out my hands to a disobedient and obstinate people.'
Sometimes the period of knocking is lifelong. I know of
one man who heard the gospel for over sixty years. Finally
the Holy Spirit opened his heart when he was ninety-seven.
John Flavel tells of a man whose heart was opened when
he was a hundred.

Christ brings great blessings to the soul that opens to him
'If any man hears my voice and opens the door I will come
into him and sup with him and he with me.' To come into
a person signifies what we call 'mystical union'. Christ
makes himself one with the believer in his death, burial
and resurrection. All the merits of Christ's atoning death
are made over to the one who believes. When we opened
our hearts to Christ we were so involved in the drama of
it that we hardly realized what a great work of the Holy
Spirit was going on in us. Now we can look back and give
the triune God all the glory.

The gospel invitation to the thirsty (Rev. 22:17)

The fact that the Greek word for 'come' is used both to
describe the invitation to *come* to Christ and for the great
final second *coming* of Christ at the end of the world means
that there is difficulty in interpreting Revelation 22:17.
Is the whole of verse 17 an invitation? Or is the first part
a longing for Christ's return which is related to those parts
of the chapter which refer to Christ's great second coming,
namely verses 7, 12 and 20? Mounce, Morris and Barclay
(referred to for his expertise in Greek, not his theology)
take the whole of verse 17 to be invitation. Swete, Hailey,
Milligan, Hengstenberg, Seiss, Hoeksema and Lenski take
the first two 'comes' to be a breathing after Christ's coming
and then an invitation.

The flow of the verse is carried forward with the word 'and', which is correctly stressed in the Authorized Version. I am persuaded that it is correct to interpret the whole verse as an invitation as this preserves the continuity and flow of thought towards the dominant feature of the verse, which is the gospel invitation to the thirsty.

The Holy Spirit says, 'Come!'

Jesus promised that he would send the Holy Spirit to convict the world of sin, righteousness and judgement. The word 'world' is used in many different ways in Scripture. For instance, in John 1:10 it is used in three ways: 'He was in the world, and though the world was made through him, the world did not recognize him.' I take the last meaning for world to be the one meant in John 16:8: 'He will convict the world,' that is, the unbelieving world. All God's elect people will be brought fully into union with Christ through the Holy Spirit's work. That does not mean that the Holy Spirit does not strive with all men. This was true in the Old Testament (Gen. 6:3). Stephen said of the Jews who listened to his last sermon before they stoned him, 'You are just like your fathers: You always resist the Holy Spirit!' (Acts 7:51). The gospel is never alone. The Holy Spirit always accompanies the gospel invitations and can convict hearers any time of the day or night. It is always true to say that God the Holy Spirit says to all the world, 'Come!' He says to all hearers, 'Come!'

The bride says, 'Come!'

The bride is the church of Christ. It is not only the individual members who invite unbelievers to come. The invitation is backed and supported by the whole assembly of believers. All are of one mind, will and longing desire — that people will pay attention to the great invitation to come to Christ. The fact that the church is a body of all kinds of people, male and female, young and old, all backgrounds and colours, all kinds of workers, greatly enhances the power of the invitation. The reason is that this factor of diversity removes the idea that the church is only for one class or kind of person. Also for every person on the outside there should be someone who will be specially able to understand and sympathize with them and to show them a welcoming attitude.

And let him who hears say, 'Come!'
Those who drink of the fountain of life for the first time are most enthusiastic about inviting all their friends to come and do likewise. We read that the woman to whom Christ spoke at the well in Samaria went and invited all the people of the town to come and hear Christ too (John 4:28–30). Would that all Christians showed this zeal! Those who love the Word of God go with enthusiasm and urgency to invite their friends. The first word used by the woman of Samaria was 'Come!' 'Come, see a man who told me everything I ever did. Could this be the Christ?'

This last invitation of Scripture is glorious in its power and universality. It is glorious too because of the unity of those who give it. Holy Spirit, bride and every hearer all say, 'Come!'

Conclusion

We have observed that the gospel invitations of the New Testament are universal, unrestricted and rich in content. They contain instructions concerning what must be done. They are presented in various ways. They come both by way of command (Acts 17:30; 1 John 3:23) and by entreaty (2 Cor. 5:21; Rom. 10:21).

This subject is of supreme importance and urgency. Therefore we should answer every objection that can be made against the freeness and fulness of the great invitation of Christ to all men everywhere. There are important subjects related to gospel preaching which if not properly understood impede the freeness of gospel invitations. We shall consider these in the next chapter.

5.
The gospel worthy of all acceptation

Andrew Fuller (1754–1815) was only twenty-seven years old when he wrote a book with the title *The Gospel Worthy of all Acceptation*. Aware of the controversy which it would cause, he delayed publication for three years. As anticipated, he faced a storm of criticism when it did appear in print. The opposition came from the hyper-Calvinists, who were obsessed with human inability to the point that they denied human responsibility. The life of Fuller is a helpful illustration of the theme of this chapter, which is that the gospel *is* worthy of all acceptation, that it *is* fully adequate and that no additions by way of 'appeals' are needed. We will be examining the principal doctrinal issues which lie behind the presentation and application of the gospel to all those who hear it.

What are these issues or key subjects?

The first is this. Since man is unable to do anything spiritually good, surely a work of the Spirit must take place in him before he has a right to believe? The answer, of course, is that no previous qualification is required. When Fuller was fifteen, he came to assurance of salvation, but this idea that he needed a qualification first hindered him. He wrote, 'I now found rest for my troubled soul; and I reckon that I should have found it sooner if I had not entertained the notion of my having no warrant to come to Christ without previous qualification.'

The next question to which an exposition will be devoted is straightforward enough, but is nevertheless important: Is man really responsible? After all, if he is spiritually unable, how can he be responsible? We must deal with that problem.

And then what about God's sincerity? If the almighty Sovereign has chosen some to salvation, has elected them and predestinated, as it says in Romans 8 and elsewhere, how can he possibly be sincere in inviting all men to come to Christ?

Related to the last subject, with respect to God's election, is the question of particular redemption. Since God has elected a people it follows that Christ died for them and effectually redeems them. If there is a limitation in God's design of redemption, surely this will restrict the free invitations of the gospel? What is the answer to that?

Again not far away from the last question is yet another, and that is the love of God. Does God love everyone? If he does not love them, then how will we be motivated to love them? This subject is vital. It deserves a full exposition.

The final consideration in this doctrinal section concerns the matter of preparation to new birth, a matter which I have handled in detail in the section on Jonathan Edwards and also explained to some extent in the chapter on the new birth. The subject of preparation is much misunderstood. For instance, it appears to contradict the fact that we need no prior qualification to believe in Christ. In actual fact there is no contradiction, providing we exercise care to observe the distinction between what we must do and what the Holy Spirit graciously works within us.

Before we begin, it will be refreshing to recall a few encouraging facts about Fuller. Converted at fifteen, he was set aside for the ministry at the very young age of nineteen. When twenty-one he was called to be pastor of the Baptist church at Soham, where he remained for eight years. At twenty-nine he was called to the Baptist church at Kettering, where he ministered for the rest of his life.

An incident occurred in his first pastorate at Soham which had a great influence upon Fuller's life. He had need to go and reprove a member of the church who was guilty of drunkenness. The man said he was unable to help himself and retaliated by accusing Fuller of being young and ignorant of the deceitfulness of his own heart. This evil distortion of the doctrine of human inability made Fuller indignant. The offending man was excommunicated, but there was considerable dissension in the church because of false thinking on the subject of inability versus responsibility.

Fuller worked hard both as a pastor and as a supporter of missionary endeavour. The membership at Kettering was 88 when he began and 174 when he died in 1815. Some might regard that as unimpressive, but the standard of church membership was much higher then and congregations in those days, in stark contrast to what they are now, were very large. Fuller had a congregation of 1,000, which is amazing when we remember that the population of the village was only 3,500. He used to preach to his own people on Sunday mornings and again in the afternoons, but the evenings were devoted to a circuit of about eight villages where he would minister to gatherings varying from fifty to five hundred. In addition to this work, Fuller toured Scotland and other parts to raise support for missionary endeavour. He was the author of several books and a prolific correspondent.

Andrew Fuller was the main instrument in his time to liberate Baptists in England from hyper-Calvinism and encourage them to return to a right biblical position. He was the intimate friend and faithful supporter of William Carey, the first Baptist missionary to India. Until the end of his life, Fuller acted as secretary of the missionary society which supported Carey in his pioneering work, which became a work of prodigious outreach by way of translation and printing in major Indian languages.

A burning issue during Fuller's lifetime was whether the sinner had the right to believe.

I   Do sinners have the right to believe?

There is much talk today of human rights. No human being can say, 'I don't have the right to believe in Christ.' By grace all are invited. In the generation preceding the time of William Carey and Andrew Fuller, there was a certain Mr Brine who maintained that it was only regenerate or born-again people whom God commanded to believe. He reasoned that God would not command what fallen sinners were unable to do.

If Mr Brine is correct in his reasoning it would mean that men could just ignore the gospel and its invitations as having nothing to do with them because they do not qualify on account of their inability.

What are we to say to that? After all, there are scriptures which endorse the hopeless state of the sinner. For instance, John 6:44 says, 'No one can come to me unless the Father who sent me draws him.' Why then should a man believe? The answer is that the sovereign God of heaven and earth commands it. This is called the 'warrant' of faith. The word warrant simply means the right to believe. This is important because many think that they must first be subject to a spiritual experience which gives them a reason or right to believe. It may be an experience of inspiration or of deep conviction of sin, but the idea is that you should experience something special before you believe. Once this erroneous concept possesses the soul, much harm is done because it means that the person in question becomes passive. Instead of thinking in terms of working for faith, the soul says to itself, 'There is nothing I can do until something happens within me.' I have come across such people who are very faithful in church attendance, but are dominated by the idea that nothing can be done by themselves. They have become fatalistic in attitude.

When the Jews asked Jesus, 'What must we do to do the works God requires?' Jesus answered, 'The work of God is this: to believe in the one he has sent' (John 6:28, 29). John states the matter very clearly when he declares, 'And this is his command: to believe in the name of his Son, Jesus Christ' (1 John 3:23). If faith is commanded and if it is a responsibility to go after it and get faith established, how should every non-Christian go about this task? Paul tells us when he declares that 'Faith comes from hearing the message' (Rom. 10:17). Intelligent attention to the preaching of the gospel message is the principal means to get faith. It is a responsibility to hear the gospel, to heed it and study it. It is a duty to discuss it with others who believe it.

Any 'hang-up', such as the false idea that leads a person

to think that the gospel is not for him because he does not have a special feeling or experience, is wrong. It destroys the urgency of the gospel and defeats its purpose. The prevalence of this is so common that we need to discuss the warrant of faith as it relates to repentance, the new birth and to the Holy Spirit.

The warrant of faith and repentance

From the Gospel of Mark it would appear that the first words preached by Jesus were 'The time has come, the kingdom of God is near. Repent and believe the good news' (that is, believe the gospel). Prior to faith is the necessity of repentance. What is repentance? *Metanoia,* the Greek word for repentance, literally means 'after-thought'. To repent is to think again, to be turned around in one's thinking, to be converted (Matt. 18:3), to turn from a wrong set of ideas to the correct framework of thought. To repent is to turn from serving this world and its idols to serve the living God. Obviously, repentance is a necessity as Jesus said, 'Unless you repent, you too will perish' (Luke 13:3).

We can distinguish between repenting (thinking again and thinking rightly) and believing (trusting the message of the gospel), but we can never separate these two essentials of repentance and faith. For instance, it is quite clear that a man is not going to believe the gospel or have anything to do with it, let alone hear preaching about it, unless there is some kind of change in his mind. He must be brought to the point where he believes that it is a gospel worthy to be listened to. And then when he does hear that gospel it is essential that he really believe it before he is prepared to do some more 'after-thinking' — changing his mind, or repenting.

We march to heaven on two feet. The one foot is called 'repentance' and the other foot is called 'faith'. Because I believe I repent about a certain sin, habit or attitude. Because I repent I return to learn more for my faith. My faith leads me to do more repentance. Left, right, left, right — one foot forward, then the other — faith and repentance, faith and repentance. This is well illustrated in

Bunyan's *Pilgrim's Progress*. In that allegory Christian
repented because the City of Destruction was so bad. He
thought again and then read his Bible. That led to faith.
Then faith led to repentance which this time led him to
leave the City of Destruction. With these two feet of repentance and faith Christian marched forward until he came
to the cross and had his sins removed. After that he went
forward to the heavenly city, repenting and believing all
the way.

One major mistake to avoid is the idea that a certain
amount of repentance has to be stored up before a person
can believe in Christ outright, once and for all, for
salvation. No! The warrant of faith for salvation is God's
command: 'Believe in the Lord Jesus, and you will be
saved' (Acts 16:31). If you give way to the notion that
a certain amount of repentance must be present before
you can have saving faith, where will that end? Who can
possibly tell whether you have done enough rethinking
or whether there is enough sorrow attached to your 'after-
thinking' or repentance about sin? If you believe that Jesus
Christ is the Son of God and that he is able and willing
to forgive you and change you, then that in itself is repentance quite adequate for you to commit yourself to Christ
wholly by faith.

The warrant of faith and the new birth

The way that our Lord dealt with Nicodemus, as recorded
in John 3, is sublime in its wisdom. Jesus took from
Nicodemus all hope of self-power, merit or ability. He
had to be born from above. Nicodemus seemed shocked
that he could contribute nothing because the new birth
is an absolutely sovereign act of God (James 1:18). But
Nicodemus was not permitted to go away with the idea
that he need not do anything. Jesus tells him all about
faith and what it is to believe. In other words, Nicodemus
is not allowed to go away muttering to himself, 'Well, there
is nothing I can do except wait and hope for the Holy Spirit
to blow upon me and give me the new birth.' Far from that,
Nicodemus has impressed firmly upon him the necessity of
believing.

Yet again we return to the fact that the warrant or right to believe is God's command. The warrant is found in God and not within ourselves. Sinners are not directed to fruitless self-examination: 'Have I, or have I not, been born again?' Nor are we ever to tolerate the idea that the warrant of faith depends upon the sinner making progress and then when he is good enough he can believe in Christ for salvation.

The warrant of faith and the Holy Spirit

Yet another 'hang-up' occurs in spiritual progress when a person thinks that he has no right to believe unless he has received the Holy Spirit. Now while it is perfectly true that sinners are powerless without the gracious enabling of God, it is equally true that he has commanded them to believe. It is foolish therefore to say to oneself, 'I cannot and will not believe for salvation, until I have evidence that I have the Holy Spirit.' No! The warrant of faith is God's command to believe. The command to believe is not prefaced with another clause or command to say that you must first have the Holy Spirit and then you may believe to salvation. What do the Scriptures say? Paul reminds the Galatian Christians that they received the gift of the Holy Spirit by believing (Gal. 3:2). They believed, and in believing the Holy Spirit was given. It is by faith that we receive the Holy Spirit (Gal. 3:14). It is not that we concentrate on the gift of the Holy Spirit and then think about faith. No! We are to concentrate on the work of believing the truth of the gospel — all of it and every part of it.

II Is man really responsible?

The teaching of the Bible is that mankind as a whole loves darkness rather than light. This is because of original sin.

And what is original sin? The Westminster Larger Catechism provides a full answer which is supported with texts: 'The sinfulness of that estate into which man fell consists of Adam's first sin, the loss of that righteousness in which he was created, and the corruption of his nature, whereby he is utterly indisposed, disabled and made opposite to all that is spiritually good and wholly inclined to all evil and that continually.' Can this be true? Note the words 'utterly indisposed' and 'disabled'. Is this not exaggerated? Not when we look at passages like John 3:19, 20, where it says men hate the light and love darkness. Here you have a double problem, a compounded difficulty. Imagine courting a girl with whom you are in love, and she says that she not only hates you (which is enough to settle it), but loves your adversary dearly! That would be final!

Major scriptures like Ephesians 2:1–10, Psalm 51 and Romans 3:10–20 confirm that man's nature is wholly unspiritual. Not passages only, but specific statements, such as 1 Corinthians 2:14 and Romans 8:7, confirm this. If man is utterly indisposed and disabled how can he be held responsible? If a sinner is dead you cannot expect him to be responsible, can you, any more than you can expect a corpse to run or jump?

To these questions I reply immediately that man is responsible. He can in no way excuse himself on the basis of inability. The word used in the catechism is 'indisposed'. Fallen man is indisposed in the sense that he does not feel like it. He has no desire and therefore has no will to be spiritual. There is nothing to hinder him from being spiritual except his indisposition, his rebellion, his sin, his unwillingness. He is absolutely free to do good, to be spiritual, to repent, to believe. That is, he is a free agent. Nobody is compelling him to do evil. He does it of his own free will. Yet there is another sense in which fallen man is not free. His will has become enslaved.

Jesus made it plain that sinners needed to be made free (John 8:32–36). Again he said, 'You will not come to me, that you might have life' (John 5:40 AV).

It could be put this way:

1. Jesus is willing to receive all who will come to him;
2. Sinners are not willing to come;
3. Sinners must be made willing to come.

Concerning the question of responsibility, A. A. Hodge put his finger on the matter when he wrote, 'Freedom of the will is an inalienable, constitutional faculty of the human soul, whereby it always exercises its volitions.' In other words, the will of man functions as it pleases. Hodge goes on to say, 'This liberty of will is essential to free agency, and is possessed by all free agents, good or bad, or they could not be held accountable.'[1]

Of course A. A. Hodge is right. Men are judged according to their accountability or responsibility. The position could be summed up like this:

1. Man is free to act as he pleases.
2. Man's pleasure is to act contrary to spiritual truth and ways and in favour of unspiritual ways.
3. This bias or prejudice of man to act contrary to the spiritual and in favour of the unspiritual in no way lessens or reduces his responsibility for all his decisions or actions. Because man is biased his will is not free towards God. Hence many, for the sake of clarity, say man is a free agent in his will, but in fact he does not have free will towards God.

That fallen man is responsible to repent and believe, and thereby be saved from guilt, condemnation and hell, is seen by the commands and invitations given to him.

When we examine the invitation of Isaiah 55 we see that those wasting their time and energy on that which does not satisfy are called to pay attention. 'Listen, listen to me, and eat what is good.' And again:

> Give ear and come to me;
>   hear me that your soul may live.

And again,

> Seek the Lord while he may be found,
>   call on him while he is near.
> Let the wicked forsake his way
>   and the evil man his thoughts.
> Let him turn to the Lord, and he will have mercy
>   on him,
>   and to our God, for he will freely pardon.

Observe the direct, plain instructions: 'Listen . . . eat . . . give ear . . . come . . . hear . . . seek . . . forsake evil . . . turn . . .'

It is absurd for the sinner to respond to these appeals by saying, 'I can't listen, eat, give ear, come, hear, seek, repent or turn!' But say the sinner does argue like that and we respond, 'Why can't you?' Is he going to say, 'I can't because I am too sinful!'?

John Bunyan makes the sinner's responsibility very clear when he describes Abraham's response to the rich man now in hell: 'Remember how thou hadst many a time the gospel preached to thee for taking away of sin. Remember that out of love to thy sins and lusts, thou didst turn thy back on the tenders of the same gospel of good tidings and peace. Remember that the reason why thou didst lose thy soul was because thou didst not close in with free grace, and the tenders of a loving and free-hearted Jesus Christ. Remember how near thou wast to turning at such and such a time, only thou wast willing to give way to thy lusts when they wrought; to drunkards when they called; to pleasures when they proffered themselves. Remember how thou, when thou wast admonished to turn, didst put off turning and repenting till another time.'[2]

Reference to Proverbs 1 confirms that Bunyan is right about the sighs and groans of hell. There are sighs and groans over opportunities lost or squandered or refused. Christ makes it plain that he called, he stretched out his hands in invitation, but he was refused. They were responsible to heed him and will be punished accordingly.

III Is God sincere in his invitations?

When the gospel invitation is made, explained, urged, reasoned, argued and pressed upon all men, a shocking discovery is made. Every person without exception makes some excuse. This fact is well illustrated by the parable of

the great banquet recorded in Luke 14:15—24. The king who prepared the sumptuous feast sent his servants to invite many guests, but they all began to make excuses:
1. I have just bought a field and must go and see it;
2. I have just bought five yoke of oxen and must test them;
3. I have just got married.

We can well understand these excuses. The modern equivalent of the oxen would be a tractor. 'I must go and test it.' It could be a new car. 'I must go and try it out!' How frivolous and offensive are these excuses! One just married is only too pleased to go and enjoy a banquet. The new house can be seen at any time and the new car can be driven at any time. The real reason is that none of these people is prepared to meet the king. He is angry with them for refusing. He wants to be kind to them, but they don't want to know.

So what does he do? He sends his servants into every corner of the land, but especially to the poor, the crippled, the blind and the lame. But how can the blind enjoy his banquet? And how will the crippled and the lame get there? Won't they also have excuses? Yes! They will also decline the invitation. Action will therefore be made to constrain them to come. 'Make them come in', says the king, 'so that my house will be full.' What does he mean? Are we to believe that the servants come back with people screaming and kicking in resistance? Surely nobody is forced to come? Rather people are made willing to accept the great invitation to the feast. We should always think in terms of the Holy Spirit taking hold of and using the means we employ to persuade people outside to heed the invitations to hear the gospel and respond to its invitations. Everywhere the Bible makes it plain that unless God acts within sinners to change them, they will never repent. It is God who quickens and raises those who are spiritually dead (Eph. 2:4—6). Salvation comes from the Lord, said Jonah. Think of Jonah when he uttered this truth. Who could possibly preserve a man inside a great fish and also retrieve that same man alive, but God? Similarly, the only way a sinner will ever be saved is by the sovereign intervention of the Almighty One. You will see from the chapter on the new birth just how much is involved in raising a spiritually dead person to life. Nobody will come to the great banquet unless God works in his soul to do so. Nevertheless this in no way reduces the effort that must be made constantly and perseveringly to bring people to the gospel feast.

We must distinguish between God's pleasure and God's will with respect to the wicked

The Bible declares clearly and unmistakably that God has no pleasure in the death of the wicked, but rather that they turn from their ways and live (Ezek. 33:11). This pleasure is in people, not an abstract principle. In other words God is declaring of any sinner whatsoever that he has no pleasure in his destruction or punishment, but rather pleasure in his turning and living. He is not saying that he is delighting in a principle as an engineer might delight in equations and formulas. This pleasure is in people personally as individuals. Now if God delights in personal salvation and has the power to regenerate sinners by giving them faith and repentance, why does he not do that for everyone and save them from outer darkness and the appalling pain of eternal fire?

The answer is that it is not his will to do so. The distinction between will and good pleasure is a valid one. It is easily understood since we constantly exercise this distinction in our lives. We can have good pleasure in many lawful comforts and pleasures, but for stern reasons may decline them and will to engage in other actions which are not pleasant but necessary in the interests of justice or discipline. We may indeed will to engage in a long and arduous course of action which is not pleasant.

It is God's will to glorify his justice in the condemnation and eternal punishment of the wicked, even though he has no pleasure whatever in it, as the Scripture says: 'What if God, choosing to show his wrath and make his power known, bore with great patience the objects of his wrath — prepared for destruction?' (Rom. 9:22.) A further passage which is helpful is Deuteronomy 29:29, where we are reminded of the distinction between the revealed will of God and the secret will of God and that there is much in this grave matter that we cannot understand.

We must realize the precious nature of grace

Grace is a precious attribute. Those who are quickened together with Christ are redeemed to the praise of the glory of God's grace. So to love an enemy as to give your life for him is an act of grace. We admire that immense sacrifice of those who lay down their lives for their country. How great is our debt to those who die to preserve the freedom of those who remain! But how do we come to terms with a man giving his life for those who spit upon him, curse him and hate him? Yet that is the nature of the grace by which we have been saved. When we understand it in these terms we could ask how it is that anyone is saved rather than why God does not save everyone.

The grace of God, like his love, has dimensions — wide and long, high and deep, and a rich character which surpasses knowledge. The incomparable riches of his grace will be shown to us in the coming ages (Eph. 2:7). We can view the basic characteristics of grace as follows:

1. The first and most fundamental characteristic of divine grace is that it presupposes sin and guilt.
2. Grace does not contemplate sinners as *un*deserving, but as *ill*-deserving.
3. Grace is not to be thought of as in any sense dependent upon the merit of its objects.
4. Grace cannot incur a debt, which is to say that it is unrecompensed. Since grace is a gift, no work is to be performed, no offering made, with a view to *repaying* God.
5. In respect to justification, grace stands opposed to works (Rom. 4:4, 5; 11:6). However, in respect to sanctification, grace is the source of works. This simply means that whereas we are saved by grace and *not* of works, we are saved by grace *unto* good works.
6. It thus comes as no surprise that in Scripture grace and salvation stand together as cause is related to effect. It is the grace of God which 'brings' salvation (Titus 2:11).
7. This grace that saves is *eternal.*
8. This grace is free, which means that man can contribute nothing towards it.
9. This grace is sovereign. If grace were at any time an *obligation* of God, it would cease to be grace.

10. Finally, grace is described in Scripture as the foundation or the means of, among other things, our election (Rom. 11:5), our regeneration (Eph. 2:5), our redemption (2 Cor. 8:9), our justification (Rom. 3:24), indeed, the whole of our salvation (Eph. 2:8).[3]

IV   How do we reconcile the doctrines of grace with the Great Invitation?

Those truths which express the fact that the salvation of sinners is an act of God are called the doctrines of grace. Probably the finest summary of these truths is that declared by Paul in Romans 8, where he defines the purpose of God. God has a purpose and we who believe have been called according to that purpose. Paul describes five links in what is sometimes called the golden chain: foreknowledge, pre-destination to be conformed to Christ, calling, justification and glorification.

The first point concerning foreknowledge is sometimes misconstrued as if God merely knew beforehand those who would choose him and therefore he chose them. That would mean a double election. When we think about that it means that God does not elect or choose at all. Man does the choosing. All that remains is for God to endorse man's choice.

It is important to see that foreknowledge in Scripture means love. Adam *knew* Eve. Jesus said, 'I *know* my sheep' (John 10:14). That does not mean that he merely knows about them beforehand. To know in such passages means to love. Election is a prominent truth in Scripture. From the beginning election was taught to young converts. It was not hidden away until some later stage. In writing to the Thessalonians the apostle has only written about sixty-four words when he tells them that they have been elected or chosen. The source of this election is love and grace (Eph. 1:4, 5; 1 Thess. 1:4). Election is a truth for which we are to be exceedingly thankful (2 Thess. 2:13). Without it nobody would be saved (Rom. 5:6).

It is not my purpose here to prove or defend the doctrines of grace, but if my reader has a problem with the subject it may be due to a lack of expository preaching. I have never found young converts rejecting these truths when they have been exposed to thorough teaching from the beginning of their Christian experience. Also it is note-worthy that election and predestination were never major issues of division in the early church. There was a mighty upheaval about the issue of circumcision and the law, so much so that a special conference was convened to debate the subject at Jerusalem (Acts 15). When it came to the sovereignty of God, Paul, in Romans 9, simply asserted the right of God to choose some to be saved. Paul was not willing to argue about the subject (Rom. 9:19).

Having had much difficulty in this matter at the beginning of my Christian experience, I do sympathize very much with those who struggle with it and who are tempted to think that election is very unfair. May I suggest that the key to accepting this biblical truth is to concentrate on the fall of man into sin as expressed in many parts of the Bible, especially Romans? When we appreciate that man is at enmity to God, has sided with Satan and always resists the strivings of the Holy Spirit (Gen. 6:3; Acts 7:51), then we marvel at the grace involved in extricating rebels from the depths of sin. We admire a mercy so great that it pro-vides everything for those who are enemies.

The question we now face is straightforward enough. If God has elected a people and predestinated them to be saved, then how can we feel free to invite everyone? To that we must add a further dimension and that is the factor of particular redemption. There are many statements which indicate that the atonement of Christ infallibly secures the redemption of his people. Two or three may be cited: 'Christ loved us and gave himself up for us' (Eph. 5:2); 'Be shepherds of the church of God, which he bought with his own blood' (Acts 20:28); 'I live by faith in the Son of God, who loved me and gave himself for me' (Gal. 2:20). These statements concur with the words of our Lord: 'I lay down my life for the sheep' (John 10:14); 'You do not believe because you are not my sheep. My sheep listen to my voice; I know them, and they follow me. I give them eternal life, and they

can never perish; no one can snatch them out of my hand'
(John 10:26–28). If, as is suggested by these and other
scriptures, Christ died for his sheep in particular, and gave
his life an effective ransom for many (Mark 10:45), not
for all, then how are we to reconcile that to the Great
Invitation which is addressed to all?

First I answer the question of election by saying that
the universal preaching of the gospel to all men of all nations
is the means of gathering in God's elect. Romans 10 stands
between two chapters which spell out the doctrines of
election and Romans 10 says, 'How can they hear without
someone preaching to them?' and 'How beautiful are the
feet of those who bring good news!' (Rom. 10:14, 15.)

Election soon becomes a great encouragement to those
who have been out evangelizing and have been discouraged
by people rejecting the gospel. There is the temptation to
think that the task is hopeless. But it is never hopeless,
because God has a purpose to save sinners. It is as we
persevere that we discover the truth expressed in Psalm
126: 'Those who sow in tears will reap with songs of joy.'

The statements of belief published at the time of the
sixteenth-century Reformation or as an outcome of that
movement are known as 'Reformed confessions'. These
statements uphold the truth of election, but at the same
time emphasize the necessity of the preaching of the gospel.
The Synod convened at Dort, Holland, in 1619 published
their beliefs in what we now know as the Canons of the
Synod of Dort. One of these declares of the gospel that
'This promise . . . ought to be declared and published to
all nations, and to all persons promiscuously and without
distinction.'[4]

We do not know who has been elected, but we do know
that a great number will be called through the preaching
of the gospel. This then gives us a great incentive to preach
the gospel to all so that many might be saved. When we
are abused or mistreated by those who hate the owner
of the vineyard (Matt. 22:6), we still comfort ourselves
in the fact that, in spite of opposition, the banqueting
hall will be filled (Matt. 22:10).

The fact that limitation exists in the atonement just
as it does in election is a question to which we now turn

our attention. As G. C. Berkouwer lucidly puts it, 'If in the predestination, "everything has been decided beforehand", has not the preacher lost his power to beckon and persuade? Will not the zeal and appealing power of the messenger become weak and eventually completely crippled?'[5] I have just shown that election, when properly understood, is the strength of the preacher, not an enervating factor, but what of the atonement, if it is limited in its efficacy to the elect?

Texts of Scripture suggesting particular atonement have already been cited. We should note concerning all these that the question concerns the issue of effectiveness. Christ's actual propitiation does accomplish its purpose of reconciliation towards God. Christ's atonement was not a matter of simply making salvation possible. It was a ransom price paid. 'He bought [us] with his own blood' (Acts 20:28). Passages such as 1 John 2:2 ('and not only for ours but also for the sins of the whole world') suggest universality, but cannot be taken to mean every single person because not everyone is saved. Rather the text points to those in every nation, tribe and kindred, and not Jewish believers only. John Owen in his monumental work *The Death of Death in the Death of Christ* expounds this verse and many others which concern the subject of the extent of the atonement. The position taken by John Owen and other expositors is that there is a sufficiency for all and a suitability for all in the atonement, so that the question of whether there is adequate provision never arises, or should never arise, in the minds of those coming to Christ.

Prof. T. J. Crawford upholds the absolute efficacy of Christ's atonement in procuring the salvation of his people according to the Father's design. Yet he firmly maintains that the gospel is to be preached to the whole world. He expresses this eloquently and we note the italics he has used for emphasis: '. . . *sufficient for all, suitable for all*, and, beyond all controversy, *pressed on the acceptance of all.* Assuredly no man has any reason or warrant to exclude himself or any of his brethren from its reference. God's *secretive will* is one of those 'secret things which belong unto himself' and which it is not for us to pry into. But God's *revealed will* 'belongs to us and to our children for ever', that we may faithfully hear it and cheerfully comply with it. And what *is* his revealed will as bearing on the matter in question? We have it clearly announced in such testimonies as the following: "These are written that ye might believe that Jesus is the Christ, the Son of God: and that believing ye might have life through his name." "This is his commandment, that we should believe on the name of his Son Jesus Christ." "Him that cometh unto me I will in no wise cast out." "God our Saviour will have all men to be saved, and to come unto the knowledge of the truth." "As I live, saith the Lord God, I have no pleasure in the death of the wicked: but that the wicked should turn from his way and live!" "[6]

We should observe, then, that the success and effectiveness of God's purpose are never to be doubted. At the same time there is never to be any inhibition in preaching the gospel to all. Rather, it is with unbounded enthusiasm that we proclaim the gospel to everyone.

V   Does God love everyone?

Does God really love everyone? Does he want everyone to be saved? If God does not really love all men, how can he command us to love them? It is certain that if we are not genuinely convinced that God *does* love everyone, our own efforts to do so will be crippled. For how can *we* pray for the highest good for people if we, in our hearts, are uncertain about whether *God* desires this highest good for them?

There are difficulties. The psalmist said that God hates the workers of iniquity (Ps. 5:5, AV). Paul says that God bears the objects of his wrath, being prepared for destruction, with great patience (Rom. 9:22). We observe the acts of God's wrath in history. Consideration of such can lead to confusion if we make false deductions. We could reason falsely that if God's wrath is revealed from heaven against all ungodliness and unrighteousness of men, then we need not interfere with that process. The first principle to observe is that as humans we are forbidden to inquire into the 'secret will' of God. 'The secret things belong to the Lord our God, but the things revealed belong to us and to our children for ever, that we may follow all the words of this law' (Deut. 29:29). Only God knows who is going to be saved. Meanwhile Scripture is clear that his love has been revealed to 'the world' in Christ (John 3:16). Secondly we know that the co-existence of the attributes of love and wrath is illustrated by our own experience. We often experience love and indignation at the same time. In fact, the more we love people, the greater is our indignation and hurt when they perform some cruel or inhuman act. If we, as limited mortals, can experience this tension, how much more the infinite God whose thoughts are as high above ours as the sky is above the earth!

When we look at the revealed purposes of God, there can be no doubt at all about this matter. God's grace is exercised towards all and is expressed by his offering the gospel to all. 'For the grace of God that brings salvation has appeared to all men' (Titus 2:11). In Romans 2:4 Paul makes it plain that the object or exercise of the riches of God's goodness applied over a long period of patience is that men might come to repentance. As we view this text we appreciate the obligation that the expressions of God's love bring to men and women. The text is rich in meaning: 'Or do you show contempt for the riches of his kindness, tolerance and patience, not realizing that God's kindness leads you towards repentance?'

The preaching of the gospel throughout the world is possible because a time of probation has been provided. During this time God shows his love, goodness and sincerity, not willing that any should perish, but that all should come to repentance. Two passages are frequently quoted in support of God's desire that all men everywhere should repent. These are important.

The first is 1 Timothy 2:4: '. . . God our Saviour, who wants all men to be saved and to come to a knowledge of the truth.' An examination of this statement within the context shows that its application to unbelievers in general is clear. It is a general statement referring to unbelievers of all kinds. We should note that it does declare God's determination to punish some sinners, such as the sons of Eli (1 Sam. 2:25).

The second passage is 2 Peter 3:9: 'The Lord is not slow in keeping his promise, as some understand slowness. He is patient with you, not wanting anyone to perish, but everyone to come to repentance.' Some insist that this text refers to believers, but that view can be challenged. Why should God's longsuffering be directed to his elect people who love and serve him? Surely, as we see in Romans 2:4, the word 'longsuffering' *(makrothumia)* is used with reference to the impenitent? In the days of Noah, God's longsuffering was directed specifically to the ungodly. He could legitimately have sent them all to a lost eternity, but he provided a time for repentance. Surely it can be argued that since it is repentance that is awaited, it is the unrepentant that are intended in the text.[7]

It is gratifying to read G. C. Berkouwer on this theme. He urges that we should take these texts as 'presented to us in the dynamic and living context of the calling to repentance and to the knowledge of the truth'. God commands all people everywhere to repent (Acts 17:30). It is in the context of the universal call that these texts come.[8]

We can call God's love for all people 'benevolent' love, a love which does good to its subjects. This is distinguished from 'complacent' love, which is that love which delights in its objects. The complacent love of God is promised by our Lord to those who keep his commandments (John 14:23, 24). It is the love expressed towards those who have been adopted as sons and daughters of God (1 John 3:2; Rom. 8:32). 'Benevolent' love is expressed towards those who are antagonistic, the unreconciled and the unrepentant. This love provides liberally so that the hearts of men and women are filled with joy (Rom. 2:4; Acts 14:17).

What are we to understand by the love described in John 3:16: 'For God so loved the world that he gave his one and only Son'? Expressed here is the wonder of God's love. He *so* loved. Two features make this love to be unique. The first is that so great a gift should be given because of this love. The second is what makes the love and love's sacrifice astonishing. It is *the world* that God so loved. What is it about this world that makes this love so great? If it was a beautiful worthy object for which God gave his supreme sacrifice, then we would not be surprised, but it is the world, in its sin, rebellion and ugliness, that God loved and sacrificed to redeem.

It is a mistake to take the meaning of 'the world' here as something referring to largeness of numbers. The context is referring to unbelief and to condemnation because men love darkness rather than light. It is the sinfulness and wickedness of the world that we are to think of. In spite of this unrighteousness, God's love prevails. Although the character of God's holiness is in complete contrast to the evil of this fallen world, yet he so loved this world, in spite of its degradation, that he gave his Son for it.

Erroneous, too, is the notion that we can make the word 'world' in John 3:16 mean all God's elect. If that was the meaning, John possessed the vocabulary to say, 'For God so loved the elect that he gave . . .' This he does not do. Nor does John say, 'For God so loved every single creature . . .' John 3:16 views the world not in terms of elect or non-elect, but as a sphere representing fallen mankind as a whole, estranged from God, far away from him, guilty and deserving just condemnation, wrath and punishment. This is a horrible world full of war, wretchedness and strife. Yet God's image is upon it. It is his handiwork and the sinners who inhabit it are made in his image. Despite its appalling character he so loves it that he gave his one and only Son, that whoever believes in him shall not perish but have everlasting life.

The character of this love is highlighted, then, both by the glory of the gift given and by the unworthiness of the world for which it was given. The character of those in the world is described in a threefold way by Paul in Romans 5. Christ died for *the ungodly,* for *sinners,* for *enemies* (Rom. 5:6–10). God's love was not deterred by the degradation and opposition of its objects.

We must now go on to observe a very important fact, which is that our love for sinners is based on God's love for sinners. Our resources of love are derived from his resources. This is precisely the force of our Lord's teaching when he said, 'You have heard that it was said, "Love your neighbour and hate your enemy." But I tell you, love your enemies and pray for those who persecute you, that you may be sons of your Father in heaven. He causes his sun to rise on the evil and the good, and sends rain on the righteous and the unrighteous. If you love those who love you, what reward will you get? Are not even the tax collectors doing that? And if you greet only your brothers, what are you doing more than others? Do not even pagans do that? Be perfect, therefore, as your heavenly Father is perfect' (Matt. 5:43—48).

The immense, unmeasured, uncalculating free love of God to all is expressed here by Christ. We are to show this loving spirit to all non-Christians and to desire with all our hearts that they should come to salvation. The motivation and strength to show real love for those outside the church is surely found in God himself. If he does not love them, we cannot expect to find the resources in him for us to love them!

God demonstrated his love for the world through the incarnate Christ. God became man, to show his love for sinners. 'God did not send his Son into the world to condemn the world, but to save the world through him' (John 3:17).

But Christ is now ascended. How is God to show his love to unbelievers now, if not through Christ's people, the church? This places a heavy responsibility on all Christians to show love to outsiders. We profess to invite men and women to repent and believe and accept God's loving invitation of forgiveness. Such invitations will be hollow and unconvincing if extended by Christians who in all practical terms show no concern whatsoever for those invited. How can people see and experience the love of God for them in Christ, if not through Christians? Christ is *in* his people and we are to demonstrate that everyday, time-consuming, patient compassion and genuine interest in people which is true love. Our fellowship as Christians is precious. But if we jealously and neurotically guard it as a 'closed shop' — something to which outsiders cannot be admitted for fear that it will be 'spoiled' — then we deny the principle of grace. God has accepted and loved us, while we hated him. We are to show love and acceptance of others and make them welcome, however awkward or socially embarrassing they are.

A pastor described to me the experience he had with a most rebellious youth who often caused chaos and disorder among the young people. His evil conduct and rebellious behaviour were a trial. Often this pastor and his wife were tempted not to pick up this young man, but since he was always willing to come to meetings, they decided to persevere. Eventually he was converted and became a great asset to the fellowship. Has not this kind of grace been seen many times in our churches? We do not know who will be saved. If the Lord shows his love by persevering, so should we.

Not only should we point to God's love in providence (Rom. 2:4), but especially and always to the immense provision of salvation in the cross of Christ. I would put it like this: Every beautiful thing, every star, every flower — *everything* that is good points to him who is the Chief of ten thousand, the altogether glorious Saviour. To him all men are invited this day.

> See him set forth before your eyes
> That precious, bleeding sacrifice!
> His offered benefits embrace,
> And freely now be saved by grace.

VI Does God prepare sinners for the new birth?

We come now to a subject in which we are confronted not with one tension, but two! In chapter 2 the problems of reconciling or accepting all the implications of divine sovereignty and human responsibility were discussed. Before we come to grapple with preparationism it is necessary to be truly conversant with the theme that there is a work the sinner must do himself, and there is a work that only God can do in the sinner. That is the first tension we will look at.

The second concerns the immediate and ongoing responsibility of the sinner, which we will examine presently.

Man is responsible to make himself a new heart (Ezek. 18:31). He may not opt out of his responsibility and say to himself, 'I'm not going to try and do anything because only God can give me a new heart. Only God can regenerate me.'

Here there is a tension which is undeniable. Only God can save me; I must save myself. God is the sole author of the new birth (James 1:18; Titus 3:5); yet at the same time Jesus says, 'Strive to enter in at the strait gate' (Luke 13:24, AV); 'Make every effort to enter through the narrow door' (NIV). The Greek word for *'strive'* is 'agonize' *(agonizesthe)*. The word is an imperative, a command. Peter commanded the same action in effect, when he said, 'Save yourselves from this corrupt generation!' (Acts 2:40.) It is plain that the new birth must come from above, that is from God alone, but at the same time the seeker is to strive to enter in at the narrow door. The tension is inescapable.

J. C. Ryle, the famous first Bishop of Liverpool, preached on Luke 13:24 and explained that the narrow gate is the only one by which sinners can get to heaven. He explained the word 'strive' as an expression which points to human responsibility: 'A man must use means diligently.'[9] Ryle also asserted that *'Strive* teaches that laziness in religion is a great sin,' and that *'Strive* teaches us that it is worthwhile for a man to seek salvation.'

What would 'striving' or 'agonizing' include? In chapter 3 we looked at the imperatives found in Isaiah 55: 'Listen ... seek . . . pray'. Our Lord confirmed those commands with similar imperatives: *'Ask . . . seek . . . knock'* (Matt. 7:7, 8). Wherever we turn in Scripture, we find that there is the work that God must do in the sinner and there is the work that the sinner must do himself. This tension continues after conversion and is evident when Paul writes in Philippians 2:12, 13, 'Continue to work out your salvation with fear and trembling, for it is God who works in you to will and to act according to his good purpose.' I will not digress to develop the believer's experience of this tension, but refer again to the pre-conversion tension and note that a perverse mind can easily ridicule this subject and say it is nonsense. To abuse this truth is an easy matter. However, we must not compromise. We must hold our ground. Remember that Nicodemus was baffled by our Lord's teaching on the new birth. 'How can these things be?' he asked. We must not be disconcerted because of these tensions of truth. If someone says, 'This will blow my mind!' we must counsel that person to be patient.

We will now examine a further tension which concerns immediate duty and ongoing duty. There is no contradiction of truth when we urge sinners to repent and believe immediately without delay (which is always their responsibility), but at the same time urge them to fulfil other duties. These duties are Bible reading, listening to expository preaching, keeping company with Christians and quitting sinful practices. There is a tension here because it seems as though we are compromising by not insisting on immediate repentance and faith.

At this point we can use an illustration. It is our custom to urge sinners to fly to Christ now. He is our only city of refuge. When the Jews occupied Canaan some cities were designated cities of refuge, where magistrates were appointed to maintain justice in cases of homicide. That is where we get the picture of Christ being our city of refuge. To reach such a city would take some time. Likewise it takes time for sinners to come to Christ. We would like them to come this very instant and, indeed, it is the responsibility of the sinner to repent and believe immediately. If he fails to do that it does not mean for one moment that he can abandon all his other responsibilities. It is a constant responsibility to attend what we call 'the means of grace' — that is the means established by God for our spiritual good. What are these means by and through which God gives his favours or grace? There is the reading of Scripture and the use of a tremendous array of fine Christian literature. There is the setting aside of time every Lord's Day to take full advantage of expository preaching, because faith comes by hearing the Word of God. There is the company of Christians and the benefit of being with them when they pray.

Human accountability is comprehensive and it is never right to compromise and say to ourselves, 'In my sphere of responsibility, I have not attained to what I should, therefore I do not care and will just accept that I am a reprobate. I will abandon all hope and cease all attempts at striving to enter the narrow gate,' or, to use the former picture, 'I have not reached the city of refuge today, therefore I will not try tomorrow.'

With regard to human responsibility, we may refer to a parallel in the realm of family responsibility. There are many aspects of family life in which a person may fail. Does failure mean that a woman should abandon her responsibilities and become an alcoholic or drug addict? Does failure mean that a man should opt out of all his responsibilities and become a tramp? If a young person fails his exams, does that mean that he should commit suicide? Satan reasons along those lines in seeking to drag men and women down. By contrast, the Holy Spirit always points to recovery, to responsibility and the pathway of repentance. Even with Cain, who turned out to be a reprobate, the Lord said, 'If you do right, will you not be accepted?' (Gen. 4:7.)

This subject is beautifully set out by one of the Puritan pastors, William Greenhill, who wrote an extensive commentary on Ezekiel. A study of that prophet led Greenhill to preach a sermon on Ezekiel 18:32: 'Wherefore turn yourselves, and live ye.' The title of that sermon is apt: 'What must and can persons do towards their own conversion'.[10] Greenhill discusses the limited powers of fallen man, particularly what he calls his 'obediential power'. The Scripture tells of man's impotency. He cannot be subject to God's law (Rom. 8:7), cannot please God (Rom. 8:8), cannot come to Christ (John 6:44), can do nothing spiritual without Christ (John 15:5), cannot believe (John 12:39; 5:44), cannot do good (Rom. 3:12; Jer. 13:23), cannot yield good fruit (Matt. 7:17) and cannot think spiritual thoughts (2 Cor. 3:15). Inability does not provide fallen man with an excuse. He cannot contract out of his moral responsibility by pleading inability.

Greenhill makes some fine observations. He suggests that the Lord calls for human endeavour. God would have all men do more than what they do perform. They can do more. While human endeavours in no way earn merit or contribute towards that power which God exerts in saving men, yet they are required to act according to what is right and true.

Greenhill observes that all that men do before their conversion is not vain or futile. It does serve a useful purpose, because it aids the means of grace which the Holy Spirit employs.

Unconverted men may in material terms do what the converted do, claims Greenhill. They may attend the means of grace and they may seriously consider the nature of their sin. They can justify the law of God by saying it is right, even if they hate the way it condemns them. Unconverted men can be conscientious rather than lazy and careless about the means of grace set before them. These means are designed for the eternal well-being of souls by the divine Surgeon, who is able to use those means for their salvation. Multitudes of unconverted people have been persuaded to continue attending church and have done so with chafing and grumbling, but have been converted in the process. Many unconverted people have been persuaded to buy and read a modern translation of the Bible and this has been instrumental in their conversion.

Preparation by God

Having examined the accountability of man and the tension that exists in the fact that he is always under obligation to repent and believe immediately, as well as under obligation to be faithful in all other spheres of his responsibility, we now concern ourselves strictly and only with what God himself does in preparing people for conversion. Jonathan Edwards observed in detail how God prepared people before the new birth (see chapter 10). Also the prince of the Puritans, John Owen, opened up this subject in detail in his book on the person and work of the Holy Spirit.[11]

Preparation before new birth can be illustrated by Ezekiel's vision of the valley of dry bones. Ezekiel was required to preach to bones first, even though that seemed to be an exercise in futility. However, the bones came together. Flesh, sinew, skin and hair were put upon the bodies, but they were still corpses. The word 'breath' is the same as the word 'spirit' in the Hebrew. It was evidently the work of the Holy Spirit to prepare these bodies for life. Ezekiel was obliged to go on preaching: 'Then he said to me, "Prophesy to the breath; prophesy, son of man, and say to it, 'This is what the Sovereign Lord says: Come from the four winds, O breath, and breathe into these slain, that they may live.'" So I prophesied as he commanded me, and breath entered them; they came to life and stood up on their feet — a vast army' (Ezek. 37:9, 10).

The ultimate animation of soul came with the breath. All that preceded was preparatory, consisting of the re-organization of the bones and the provision of the sinews, the organs, the flesh, the skin and the hair.

So it is with conversion. No one has any patience to listen to the gospel, to hear about Christ, let alone actually come to Christ, unless there is the powerful drawing of the Father (John 6:44). The Day of Pentecost can be likened to Ezekiel's vision of the valley of dry bones. Several thousand had been drawn at great expense and from long distances to Jerusalem. To a large extent they had been taught. They had been prepared. They knew the Scriptures well. We see that because Peter had the advantage of being able to quote Joel to them in detail and expound the fulfil-ment of Psalms 16 and 110. They were not clueless, ignorant Gentiles. They were earnest proselytes, keen learners, many of whom had erred miserably in following the Jewish leaders in rejecting Christ and agreeing with his crucifixion.

Similarly, when we examine the conversion accounts of others in the book of Acts we discover that to some degree or other they were prepared. The Ethiopian eunuch was a student of Isaiah who had been led to the most relevant passage of all. Philip was called to enlighten him. The Samaritans heard the preaching first; then they believed (Acts 8:12). Saul was fighting against the truth and perse-cuting the church before he was converted (Acts 9:5).

Cornelius, the centurion, is portrayed as a devout, God-fearing man. He was a generous giver and prayed to God regularly. The description would place him in the category of Abraham and the company of all the devout Jews involved in the period of transition from the old dispen-sation to the new. They bore the marks of the new birth and therefore embraced the truth of Jesus immediately it was presented to them.

It is very difficult to tell the exact moment of new birth. We may be able to guess more or less. We can observe a change in people. Often their very faces seem different, but to pinpoint the moment is like trying to pinpoint the wind.

It is fascinating to study the different examples of conversion in the Bible. Of them all we have to say that faith and salvation are preceded by knowledge (Rom. 10:14). While we cannot locate the precise moment of new birth, we can observe the transition from darkness to light. It is possible to observe the convictions antecedent to transformation and then watch the new life that blossoms after regeneration.

In Acts 16 we are confronted with the contrast of Lydia on the one hand and the Philippian jailer on the other. Lydia was already prepared, devout, receptive and believing. The jailer, by comparison, was a violent unbeliever, ready to commit suicide in a time of severe crisis. Where is preparation to be found in the jailer or, in fact, in the dying criminal crucified alongside Jesus? All we can say is that there was some prior accumulation of knowledge and that the work proceeded at great speed.

Preparation outlined by way of illumination, conviction, reformation

Before we proceed to these points, it will help to observe that there is a work of the Holy Spirit that falls short of regeneration. King Saul prophesied by the Spirit, as did Balaam, but both of them proved to be reprobate. Hebrews 6:4–6 speaks of 'those who have been once enlightened, who have tasted the heavenly gift, who have shared in the Holy Spirit, who have tasted the goodness of the word of God and the powers of the coming age'. We can readily see from this that there are those who are illuminated but not regenerated. It can be put like this: all who have been regenerated have been illuminated, but not all those who have been illuminated have been regenerated. Hebrews

10:26 tells of receiving a knowledge of the truth, while verse 29 tells of being sanctified (set apart) by the blood of the covenant. All this can transpire without the person being born again. Likewise, in the parable of the sower our Lord speaks of the seed sown in rocky places. It springs up, but there is no depth of soil. There are those who receive the Word with joy, but this lasts a short time only, and when trouble and persecution come, they fall away. It seems clear enough that it is possible to partake of the Holy Spirit, but not to be born again of the Holy Spirit. So Peter describes those who go so far in a work of reformation in their lives that they escape the corruption of the world by knowing our Lord and Saviour Jesus Christ, yet afterwards are entangled by the world and overcome, their last state being worse than before they ever began (2 Peter 2:20).

Our concern now is with that work of the Holy Spirit which does actually prepare a soul and bring it to new birth. Since nobody can be converted without a knowledge of what he is being converted to, this presupposes content and teaching prior to the new birth which is used by the Spirit to illuminate or enlighten a person's mind.

Illumination

The contrast between children who have grown up in Christian homes and have from their earliest years been saturated with Christian teaching and those who are wholly outside the church is enormous. A comprehensive knowledge of the Bible is possessed by the one, while the other is ignorant. It is because of this ignorance that the majority today show contempt for the gospel. Having come, through the brainwashing of popular mythology, to believe that the Bible merely consists of stories for children, they are impatient and wonder how people can take the Bible seriously. Evolution is accepted as fact and the miraculous automatically rejected as scientifically untenable. Thus blinded to the truths of the gospel and always predisposed to reject any consideration of them, they are doomed to eternal destruction – apart, that is, from a divine intervention.

By contrast, how privileged are those who grow up with Christian values! They have a framework of knowledge which enables them to accept the supernaturalism of the Bible as consistent with its Author. Their problems are seldom intellectual. They do not reject the truth as such, but simply remain unmoved by it. There are peculiar dangers that beset those born into the environment of gospel nurture and practice, namely complacency in the knowledge they possess and the tendency to procrastinate with regard to coming to Christ personally. There is also the tendency to rest in the general care and protection afforded them by their Christian guardians. Often the children of privilege learn to enjoy good preaching, yet at the same time develop the art of keeping away anything which directly challenges their state of non-reconciliation to the Father through repentance of sin and faith in Christ.

A frequent temptation which Satan brings to the children of believers is for them to think that their religious ties are disadvantageous and an embarrassment which they could well do without. Such excuses can be dealt with by explaining such texts as 2 Timothy 3:15: 'From infancy you have known the holy Scriptures, which are able to make you wise for salvation through faith in Christ.'

This appeal to the instrumentality of Scripture illustrates the fact of preparations by Scripture. We have to know who Christ is before we can believe upon him. How can a person be taught without substance, or be convicted of need without the substantiation of facts? That leads to our next consideration with regard to preparation for new birth.

Conviction

It is usual for God to make sinners aware of their guilt and danger before he reveals his love and mercy to them. The Philippian jailer was acutely aware of his lostness and hopelessness before he received mercy. The prodigal son was brought to despair before he returned home. It is often the way of God to humble souls before he saves them. He reveals to them the corruption of their hearts, their inability to do anything spiritual and their bondage to besetting sin before he gives them the joy of justification and the delight of deliverance from the power of enslaving sin. If we examine the experiences of Luther, Bunyan and Spurgeon, we see that they were brought to an end of themselves before they trusted in Christ alone for salvation. In citing these examples we must take great care to avoid laying down or circumscribing the preliminaries to new birth. Some are born again after prolonged agonies and some quietly, easily and effortlessly, like the dew of the morning.

The Scripture lays stress on the place of the law to bring conviction, which is an emphasis we should not forget. Jesus confronted the rich young ruler with the Ten Commandments, especially the first and tenth commandments, in requiring that he go home and sell all. James uses the Ten Commandments (James 2:8–11), as does Paul (Rom. 13:8–11). The searching demands of the moral law are pressed home by Christ in the Sermon on the Mount (Matt. 5:17–48). It is helpful to remember that it is by the law that we have a knowledge of sin. Paul likens the law to a schoolmaster, to bring us to Christ (Gal. 3:24, 25, AV). The law to which he refers is the whole law, including its ceremonial aspects, which were designed to show just how exacting it was for atonement to be made for sin before a holy God. Everything in Scripture which reveals human bankruptcy and Christ's fulness is helpful to assist the advance of conviction. The Holy Spirit is promised as the person who will convince the world of sin, of the need of righteousness and of the certainty of judgement to come (John 16:7–11).

In these days it is difficult to arouse any sense of sin or guilt, so that when anybody does get conviction we tend to conclude too much from it. Conviction is not conversion. Past spiritual awakenings have it on record that some who showed very great conviction of sin in due course went back. This highlights the danger of assuring people that they are saved when the evidences and fruits are lacking and when there has been inadequate time to see if they will show perseverance. A letter was screened on television in which a former 'convert' derided Christianity. He declared that he had been converted twenty years ago. For ten years he lived as an evangelical Christian and thereafter as an atheist. This proves, he said, that Christians can't fool all their people all the time! All that person was doing is proving the truth of the Bible that only those who persevere to the end are saved, or, as John puts it, 'They went out from us, but they did not really belong to us. For if they had belonged to us, they would have remained with us; but their going showed that none of them belonged to us' (1 John 2:19).

Souls under conviction should be directed with scriptural directives. Our Lord laid great emphasis on seeking. He never employed a simple formula, after the fashion of some evangelistic enterprises, in two, three or four easy steps. 'Seek first the kingdom' (Matt. 6:33); 'Ask and it will be given to you; seek and you will find; knock and the door will be opened to you' (Matt. 7:7). Times when the Holy Spirit is evidently at work are especially propitious. As Isaiah expressed it, 'Seek the Lord while he may be found: call on him while he is near' (Isa. 55:6). Also stressed by our Lord is the invitation to come to him. 'Come to me, all you who are weary and burdened' (Matt. 11:28). 'If a man is thirsty, let him *come* to me and drink' (John 7:37).

But how do you come? To call on the Lord is to pray to him and to pray to him is to draw near to him. 'Take words with you and return to the Lord. Say to him: "Forgive all our sins and receive us graciously"' (Hosea 14:2). We should therefore encourage our unconverted seekers to pray. Indeed, without prayer nobody can ever come to God, as it says in Psalm 65:2:

> O you who hear prayer,
> to you all men will come.

It is the will of God to give his mercy to those who call on him for it. 'Everyone who calls on the name of the Lord will be saved' (Rom. 10:13). That guarantee that the Lord will richly bless all who call on him should not be oversimplified, for the call has to come from a truly seeking heart, as we are reminded by the words: 'Then you will call upon me and come and pray to me, and I will listen to you. You will seek me and find me when you seek me with all your heart' (Jer. 29:12, 13).

Of course, there are some who think it foolish to exhort the unconverted to pray, on the basis of the text that 'The sacrifice of the wicked is an abomination to the Lord' (Prov. 15:8, AV). This view, however, is unbalanced. We should note that there are degrees of sin, as we see from similar statements:

> The sacrifice of the wicked is detestable —
> how much more so when brought with evil intent!
> (Prov. 21:27)

> If anyone turns a deaf ear to the law,
> even his prayers are detestable
> (Prov. 28:9).

These verses apply to gross hypocrites. The curse of a divided heart is found to some degree in all believers and this guarantees that sin is mixed with all they do, even with their prayers. We may struggle to pray because of our sinfulness, but not to pray at all is a greater sin. So with the unconverted: not to repent, not to believe, not to pray is to guarantee disaster. To seek to repent and believe, even though there is a divided heart, is to head in the direction of salvation. To attempt to use the means of grace laid before him is the responsibility of every sinner. His inability can never be used as an excuse, because he must look to God for help. He must turn to the one in whom all power and grace resides. From God, the infinite fountain of all goodness, the sinner may obtain upon request full supplies of needed ability for spiritual actions.

We have seen that knowledge is essential. God prepares sinners for regeneration by giving them illumination, by showing them the meaning of biblical truth. By nature they are opposed to that (Rom. 8:7,8) and can never grasp it (1 Cor. 2:14), but God reveals truth to them and convicts them of need. Even that is not enough. There must be reformation.

Reformation

Closely allied to illumination and conviction is reformation of life. As knowledge increases, together with persuasion that the gospel is true, so response is reflected in a person's way of life. We know that the Holy Spirit can work suddenly without such preparation, but mostly he prepares souls by drawing them into the Christian circle. On a wide scale this can be seen in families. Those born into Christian families are born into an environment which God uses to prepare them to salvation. The disciplined way of life to which they become accustomed is conducive to the spiritual life which follows regeneration. In the same way the Holy Spirit moves in nations or groups of people. A general sympathy for the means of grace in a community often precedes a spiritual awakening. Conversely, the situation looks hopeless for whole nations which are locked up in Islamic lands where hostile attitudes and laws are maintained towards anything at all which promotes the gospel. Of course, the Holy Spirit works in spite of such adverse conditions, in the salvation of individuals, but my general observation holds.

On the personal level, the main point to note is that often people reform their way of life considerably before they are converted. They give up idolatrous practices, begin to attend church regularly, cease to blaspheme and avoid sins which they know will be harmful to their spiritual progress.

Conclusion

Since God prepares people for conversion by way of the means just expounded, it is important that we do not give way to the idea that we can force the issue at any time. We must not think that by creating the right atmosphere and making an 'appeal', followed by a set form of counselling, we can produce the new birth. The Holy Spirit is sovereign. He who prepares souls for the new birth will do his work in his own time and not our time. It is good to recall those famous words through Zechariah: ' "Not by might nor by power, but by my Spirit," says the Lord Almighty' (Zech. 4:6).

We must learn to live with the tensions that exist in the

gospel, the tension of God's sovereignty and human responsibility, as well as the tension that the immediate duty for the sinner to repent and believe does not negate in any way other ongoing responsibilities. I have spent more time on this theme of preparationism because it is so little understood and also because so many sincere people are confused about it. Many deny one truth or the other, or stress one aspect at the expense of the other. Happy is that believer who appreciates these divinely profound issues!

Footnotes
1.   A. A. Hodge, *The Confession of Faith*, Banner of Truth, p. 260.
2.   John Bunyan, *A few sighs from hell, or the groans of a damned soul*, Offer edition, vol. 3, p. 690.
3.   This ten-point outline is based on that provided by C. Samuel Storms, *The Grandeur of God*, Baker, 1984, p. 124.
4.   *Canons of Dort*, II, 5.
5.   G. C. Berkouwer, *Divine Election*, Eerdmans, p. 218.
6.   T. J. Crawford, *The Atonement*, 1883, p. 202.
7.   For a discussion of the exegesis of 2 Peter 3:9 see *Reformation Today*, No. 38, p. 37.
8.   G. C. Berkouwer, *Divine Election*, Eerdmans, p. 238.
9.   J. C. Ryle, *Practical Religion*, James Clark, 1970, p. 22.
10. Puritan Sermons 1659–1689, Cripplegate London, 6 vols., Richard Owen Roberts, 1981, vol. 1, p. 38.
11. John Owen, *Works*, Banner of Truth, vol. 3, p. 228 ff.

6.
The history of the invitation system

In chapter 1 we considered the prevalence of the use of the 'appeal', or 'altar call' today. Following that we explored the biblical parameters of what is involved in the invitations of the gospel. We also investigated the doctrines related to the subject. Now we concern ourselves with the origins and history of the 'appeal'.

In an article printed in an early *Banner of Truth Magazine* (No. 32) Albert B. Dod, a one-time professor of theology at Princeton Seminary, made the claim that the practice of urging people to come forward at the end of the preaching services was introduced by Charles G. Finney (1792–1875). Dod asserted that this method was without historical precedent. This view has been widely held, but is now being strongly challenged. For instance, it is disputed in the book by Alan Streett (see chapter 1).

In his study, *The Effective Invitation,* Streett suggests that the invitation system was in vogue before and after Constantine. He shows tremendous enthusiasm for the 'appeal', but unfortunately imports the method, as well as our modern evangelical culture and outlook, back into history. So extravagant are some of Streett's suggestions that you can almost envisage Constantine himself making his way down the aisle to grasp the hand of a crusade evangelist while the choir sings, 'Just as I am'! To Streett, descriptions of powerful preaching, such as that of Chrysostom,[1] or reports of many converts, as in the case of Boniface,[2] indicate the use of the invitation system. Streett refers to Bernard of Clairvaux (1093–1153), who he claims used to call for a show of hands for those who wished to be restored to the church or to fellowship with God. Streett does not give original, only secondary references. This casts doubt on the value of his work.

The Reformers and Puritans did not know of the 'appeal'. They did not attempt to create anything of that kind. Streett admits this. It is when we reach the eighteenth century in Streett's brief survey of church history that we have to take him more seriously. He tells of a Jesuit priest, Jacques Bridaine (1701–1767), who he suggests may be the first man in modern history to practise effective mass evangelism. He attracted large numbers in France by using processions, music and large banners to advertise his meetings. To quote Streett, 'His co-operative efforts with local priests were most successful.' The historian Edwin Dargan is cited by Streett as saying that Bridaine called for 'public avowals of renewed faith or of first confessions of Christ'.[3] Before we think in terms of predating Finney's methods by a century, we should remember that Roman Catholic priests have been notorious for applying baptismal regeneration *en masse*.

As we go on into the eighteenth century, we find several claims that the invitation system was used. For the sake of clarity we will investigate and discuss them under the titles of the various leaders or preachers involved. Methods arose to deal with unusual circumstances and we have to be cautious about that tendency which seizes incidents to illustrate a system which has developed to become a regular routine. Revival is extraordinary and events in revivals do not form a norm for practice. The eighteenth century is remembered as the time of the Great Awakening, the era of Whitefield and the Wesleys. Anyone who doubts the reality of revival should read Arnold Dallimore's *Life of Whitefield* to realize the immense power of the Holy Spirit outpoured during those years in Britain and America. With these observations we turn now to an event which is made much of by Kendall in his book.[4]

Eleazar Wheelock (1711–1779)

1741 was a year in which the Great Awakening was at flood-tide. It was a time when Jonathan Edwards preached his famous sermon, 'Sinners in the hands of an angry God'. If you look on the map you will see that Northampton, Massachussetts is not far from Connecticut. At Lebanon, Connecticut, Eleazor Wheelock was preaching. An eyewitness provided the following description: 'As he was delivering his discourse very pleasantly and moderately, the depth and strength of feeling increased, till some began to cry out both above and below, in awful distress and anguish of soul, upon which he raised his voice, that he might be heard above their outcries; but the distress and outcry spreading and increasing, his voice was at length so drowned that he could not be heard. Wherefore, not being able to finish his sermon, with great apparent serenity and calmness of soul, he called to the distressed, and desired them to gather themselves together in the body of the seats below. This he did, that he might the more conveniently converse with them, counsel, direct, exhort them, etc. But he ought not to have done it . . . He should have sent his hearers home, to engage in solitary, serious thought, in reading.' The eyewitness himself was not happy with the idea of calling the distressed forward. Unfortunately we do not know his reasons.

What are we to say about it? My response is one of sympathy. From this account I would rejoice to see such concern seize a congregation and would certainly wish to counsel the people as much as possible and to be assisted in that way by mature Christians capable of providing solid biblical direction on a one-to-one basis. Whitefield was accustomed to counselling souls awakened by his ministry. Any reader of his *Journals* can check that for himself.

We should be careful to note that no formal procedure was being established. Nothing would please a normal evangelical minister more than many people coming under a deep sense of conviction of sin and having to improvise in order to help them. Surely that is basic to every genuine revival. Only sheer exhaustion would excuse a minister for leaving a scene of distress and then he would arrange to see the people at a further gathering.

R. T. Kendall shows considerable excitement about this discovery and makes much of the fact that the invitation system was born in a time of revival. He stresses this and drives it home.[5] This particular revival was a thrilling event, but it does not follow that the means employed by Wheelock to solve a particular problem should now have divine authority. Simply because a measure or means is used in exceptional circumstances does not mean that it must be instituted as an approved procedure. We do not know what Wheelock practised subsequent to that incident. I do not believe that he himself regarded calling people to the front as a new method for use by the churches.

George Whitefield (1714–1770) and John Wesley (1703–1791)

In his *Journals,* Whitefield describes many occasions when many sought him for spiritual counsel — many, that is, who were distressed on account of conviction of sin. There is no evidence that Whitefield set up a counselling system. Rather, with the co-operation of his friends and supporting ministers, he sought to deal efficiently with every different occasion or situation.

From all accounts, despite his differences with Whitefield over the doctrines of grace, John Wesley maintained the same insistence on the necessity of genuine repentance as did Whitefield. Wesley insisted on holiness of life and he disdained nominal Christianity. He laid down rules for the Methodist societies. Streett maintains that John Wesley invited seekers to step up to the front and publicly present themselves for church membership. I have searched Wesley's works, but found no reference to an anxious seat or a mourners' bench. Wesley had a voluminous correspondence and someone may be able to locate references to this matter. He may well have employed the practice, but before we can examine the matter in its context we would first need to have the documentation.

If historical research concerning Wesley himself produces nothing tangible, then there still remains a large corpus of literature on Methodism. Streett recounts that Lorenzo Dow, a well-known Methodist evangelist, developed a progressive invitation, first by asking for those who wished their souls to be prayed for to stand. Dow then invited all seekers immediately to move to the front for prayer. He also refers to a Methodist camp meeting at Red River, Kentucky, where an altar was erected in front of the pulpit 'designed as a place for penitents, where they might be collected together for prayer and instruction'.[6]

To sum up to this point, it would seem that revivals varying in intensity continued towards the end of the eighteenth century and on into the nineteenth century, and that a variety of methods were used to gather the distressed in order to counsel them. We should emphasize that the purpose was to advise and help those who were distressed. There are no reports of methods employed to encourage people to come forward at the conclusion of meetings.

Charles Grandison Finney (1792–1875)

Finney is an important person in the history of the church. He is regarded by some of his admirers as America's greatest revivalist. Because of his Pelagian theology and the methods he invented, many regard him as a disastrous influence on ensuing generations of evangelical Christians.

Finney began practising law at the age of twenty-six. At the age of twenty-nine he was converted and claimed soon afterwards to have intense experiences called 'the baptism of the Spirit'. He then studied theology under a conservative Presbyterian minister, George W. Gale. When the Presbyterians with hesitation licensed Finney to preach he had still not read the Westminster Confession of Faith. All Presbyterian ministers were and are supposed to sub-scribe to this confession.

A women's missionary society supported Finney on a missionary tour of Jefferson county. He is reputed to have had great success there and in other places which marked the beginning of his revival ministry.[7] His work proceeded steadily, but it was not until a campaign in 1830 in Rochester, New York State, that his fame spread on a large scale. For six months he could dominate the religious life of a large city. He secured the co-operation of most of the churches. It was from this time on that Finney mostly used the mourners' bench as a method in his evangelism. In 1832 Finney became the minister of Chatham Street Chapel in New York City. He broke with the Presbyterians and organized his church along Congregational lines. His responsibilities increased when he began to serve as a professor of theology at the new college in Oberlin, Ohio. The college classes were held in summer, which freed Finney to fulfil his pastoral commitments in New York for the rest of the year. He resigned his New York pastorate in 1837 and took on a pastorate at Oberlin, where he remained until 1872.

In addition to this he conducted frequent evangelistic campaigns in various parts, the most notable being four at Boston, including one in 1841–42, known as the Great Boston Revival. Twice he visited Britain, in 1849–50 and 1858–59. Finney was hostile to Reformed theology. Just how opposed Finney was to the doctrine of original sin, the imputation of Christ's righteousness and the biblical doctrine of regeneration, is well documented by J. F. Thornbury in his book *God Sent Revival*.[8] To him conversion was the direct result of moral persuasion by the appropriate use of means. Success by way of numbers was important. This, as far as he was concerned, was a decisive proof that God was in it. He was quite radical in his pragmatic approach to evangelism. In order to multiply conversions Finney introduced what came to be known as 'new measures'. These included the 'anxious bench'. This was a pew at the front of the church or hall where those who were 'repentant and eager to turn to God' were invited to come. It was at Rochester that this measure was first introduced.

Two well-known ministers, Dr Lyman Beecher at Boston and Asahel Nettleton, were opposed to Finney's methods. Nettleton believed that Finney was sowing the seeds of fanaticism. The mourners' bench was not the last point of reference in a meeting because Finney would often gather the penitents into an 'enquiry room' for counselling.

Details of Finney's life have been described because I regard him as the catalyst for modern evangelistic methods. It is Finney who marks the watershed of a new era for city-wide modern evangelism and the invitation methods that are used. The American historian Sydney E. Ahlstrom describes Finney as 'an enormously successful practitioner, almost the inventor of the modern high pressure revivalism which, as it spread, would have important consequences for the religious ethos of the nation as a whole'.[9]

The basis of this evangelism was Finney's view of man's natural ability to repent and believe. Thus there was a tremendous emphasis on the need to press for immediate decisions. If it is true, as Finney believed it was, that conversion merely depends on our powers to persuade the sinner, who is supposedly free, then where does the mighty power of God to regenerate souls fit in? And what about all that the Scriptures have to say about fallen mankind being at enmity to God? Free will is simply not true in practice and is not what the Bible says about men. Finney was a dogmatic proponent of the notion that methods produced commensurate results, in the absolute sense. The sovereignty of God in salvation exercised no power or influence in his theology, which contrasts completely with that of Jonathan Edwards, who is rightly regarded as the church's foremost theologian on revival.

Gardiner Spring, a well-known preacher and author of the last century, drew attention to two serious errors made popular by Finney. The first was the notion of praying in faith. Finney propagated the idea that God is bound by his Word. Therefore he must give us what we request. If we pray in faith we must secure what we ask. Thus at the commencement of a mission if we ask in faith for a hundred souls to be converted, then it follows that a hundred souls will be converted. If we are about to be involved in a nation-wide campaign of evangelism and we agree among ourselves to pray for 100,000 souls, then if we pray in faith for 100,000 souls, that number will be converted. This simplistic approach entirely misses the truth that we cannot know God's purposes and designs. There is a great difference between presumption and submission.

The fact is that we do not possess an analogy or correspondence of our minds with the mind of God. If we did, then we would possess the power to perform miracles in an infallible way. This is illustrated in the case of a certain Mr Pierson, who employed Finney's method of using the prayer of faith. When his wife died, he gathered his friends around the dead body of his wife, believing that the prayer of faith would raise her to life again. The outcome is predictable. In due course they were compelled to accompany the lifeless corpse to the grave. It is a form of fanaticism to presume that God must act in any way at all simply because we use a device or method which is called 'the prayer of faith'.

A second error popularized by Finney was that true converts could be identified immediately. It is fanatical and misguided to believe that we can know with certainty that people are born again in the excitement of a meeting. There is a world of difference between a credible profession of faith, which is supported by the fruits of repentance, and an on-the-spot testimony, which may well be generated by artificial stimulus. The case of Pentecost is always quoted to support the idea that we should act immediately. There were many evidences that Pentecost constituted a special occasion. Personally, I believe that Pentecost was a fulfilment of Zechariah 12:10—14. The depth of repentance was extraordinary. It was a *grief*-stricken repentance such as has characterized most powerful revivals. The repentance was 'like the weeping of Hadad Rimmon in the plain of Megiddo', likened to grief for the loss of a first-born son.

Concerning Finney we are constrained to observe that his reputation was largely the outcome or result of his fanatical ideas and practices. Finney believed that revivals were the result of concerted efforts and he believed that they could be promoted by those who possessed the requisite skills and determination. So powerful did Finney's influence become that his theology of salvation and his basic method in evangelism have become standard practice in America today.[10]

As we now consider more briefly those who followed Finney we should see more clearly the connection between him and those who in a general sense followed his ideas and his methods.

D. L. Moody (1837–1899), Sam Jones (1847–1906), Reuben A. Torrey (1856–1928) and Billy Sunday (1862–1935)

D. L. Moody was the foremost evangelist of the last quarter of the nineteenth century. Before entering the ministry he was a clerk in the boot and shoe business. In 1870, Moody became associated with Ira D. Sankey, a gospel hymn-writer who accompanied him on his tours of Britain in 1873–75 and again in 1881–83. Moody directed annual Bible conferences at Northfield, Mass., and he founded the Chicago Bible Institute. A monthly magazine as well as an evangelical publishing house bearing his name are famous in America.

Moody's method in mass evangelism was to get all those who wanted salvation to stand. Sometimes he requested that they should stand and say, 'I will!' Those standing were then urged to make their way to the enquiry room for counselling. Moody would himself descend from the pulpit and with outstretched hands persuade the people to continue rising and follow him into the enquiry room. The name and address and church of each person coming into the enquiry room would be taken and advice given by trained counsellors.

After Moody, Sam Jones was the next most famous American evangelist. Jones was a lawyer who wrecked his career because of drink, but after his conversion he became a Methodist evangelist who was as hostile to alcohol as he was to the devil. His invitation method was similar to that used by Moody.

Reuben Torrey came after Sam Jones, but did not have the same statistical success — 100,000 responses, compared with 500,000 which came from the appeals made by Sam Jones.

When Torrey got people to indicate their response by standing and saying, 'I will', he would encourage them with the words: 'God bless you'. He would then get them all to repeat the words: 'I have taken Jesus as my Saviour, my Lord and my King.' They were then requested to come and occupy seats in the front to receive instruction and engage in prayer. While this was going on, there was a further procedure, inasmuch as personal workers moved along the aisles pleading earnestly with those who had resisted Torrey's appeal. This lasted about five minutes. Many additional enquirers came forward through this method.[11]

We turn next to William Ashley Sunday, who spent four years in an orphanage. He grew up on a farm and then worked as an undertaker's assistant. Billy Sunday then became a professional baseball player from 1883 to 1891. After he became an evangelist he conducted 300 campaigns. In 1910, Sunday was at Bellingham, Washington, where there was a sawmill industry. Woodsmen used to enter thick forests and, in order not to get lost, they took with them bags of sawdust which they left as a trail to guide them back home. The sawdust trail was their guide to safety. Sunday spiritualized this as he called sinners to follow the sawdust trail right down to the front to meet with Christ. The sawdust, if liberally spread, was also useful to keep down the sound of marching boots. In his Philadelphia campaign 40,000 hit the sawdust trail! Billy Sunday is reputed to have had one million make public professions.

Sometimes with a straight face I have told fellow pastors about the time I heard and saw Billy Sunday preach! 'Well, how can that be?' is the response. In Wheaton, Chicago, there is the Billy Graham Institute or Museum for Evangelism. There is a section devoted to Billy Sunday. If you put your money in the box, you will see a brief film and hear Billy Sunday. Never in my life have I seen any preacher use his body so much or exhort with such rapid fury. I am not surprised that he got a million to hit the sawdust trail!

Billy Sunday changed his methods over the years. Earlier, he employed a progressive invitation. He would appeal for people to come forward. When the flow slowed down, personal workers would go out to exhort more to come. The next step was the choir. The director, Homer Rodeheaver, would lead inviting music. Eventually, Billy Sunday would himself address those who had come forward. He eventually simplified this procedure and opted for people to come forward and shake him by the hand and thereby signify their acceptance of Christ as Saviour. He could shake hands at a speed of eighty-four people in sixty seconds using both hands and a queue on either side. Those who came forward were given a card which stated, 'By this act of coming forward . . . you are now the child of God and you now have eternal life.' Sometimes he would say, 'Come on down and take my hand against booze, for Jesus Christ, for your flag.'

Billy Graham (1918–   )

Billy Graham was himself converted through an evangelistic campaign with Mordecai Ham as the preacher. There were wood shavings and sawdust on the floor and a handshake from the preacher. He studied at the Bob Jones University and then at the Florida Bible Institute. From the very beginning of his ministry, Billy Graham used the invitation system.

Alan Streett devotes an entire chapter in his book to the evolution and methodology of the Graham style of invitation. Dr Graham used to employ the progressive invitation up to the time of the mid-1950s. The progressive method is to get people to respond first by raising their hands and then to get them to come forward. He then changed from that to simply having all heads bowed and eyes closed for prayer and then, as an indication that individuals are giving their lives to Christ, calling them to come to the front. However, by the mid-1960s, Billy Graham was using a simple one-step invitation. He now omits the stage of heads being bowed for prayer and exhorts his hearers to simply leave their seats and make their way up to the front of the platform.

Dr Graham declares that he preaches for a verdict. A decision must be made. During the sermon there are overtures which prepare the hearers for the time of decision. For instance, reference may be made to some interesting personality who made such a life-transforming decision. A person who has desperate problems and difficulties similar to that person is encouraged thereby to decide for Christ as well. The transition from the sermon to the invitation is exceptionally smooth. It is often jarring when ministers who use this method change gear from the activity of preaching to that of endeavouring to get people to make a physical response by raising their hands or coming forward. While I agree that the transition with Dr Graham is exceptionally smooth, I have often noticed the tremendous contrast between his best preaching and the activity connected with the actual appeal. There is a transposition from one sphere of thought to another.

It is important to note that Billy Graham does not equate coming forward with salvation. According to Streett, that view is heresy and he dislikes Iain Murray's charge in his booklet *The Invitation System*, where he makes that suggestion. He quotes Dr Graham as saying that 'There's nothing about the mechanics of coming forward that saves anybody's soul. Coming forward is an open acknowledgement and a testimony of an inward experience that you have had with Christ. But this inward experience with Christ, this encounter, is the most important thing.'[12] As we will see in the next chapter, this statement presumes far too much and the whole practice is leading, or has led, to what is tantamount to a new evangelical sacrament.

Luis Palau (1934–   )

Known as 'the Billy Graham of Latin America', Palau is considered the foremost evangelist in the Spanish-speaking world.

Apparently Palau, who has a Plymouth Brethren background, had considerable difficulty at first in accepting any type of public invitation. He felt that the public appeal strives at a man's emotions, but does not change his heart or mind. When Palau began for the first time to use the appeal system he had much trepidation. Of about seventy-five people, thirty-five hands were raised in response to the request as to whether they had accorded with his prayer seeking forgiveness and inviting Jesus into their hearts.

Palau's method after preaching his message is to ask for all to bow their heads. Those who sincerely desire to receive Christ are requested to repeat silently a prayer of repentance and faith. As the choir sings, those who offered the prayer are asked to come to the front of the auditorium. This serves as a proclamation of the salvation of those coming forward. To Palau, coming forward is not an act of being saved. The act of being saved is when a person calls on the name of the Lord. Those coming forward are showing publicly that they have been saved.

R. T. Kendall (1935–   )

Before becoming the minister of Westminster Chapel, London, R. T. Kendall studied at Oxford, where he pastored a Southern Baptist church. He has written six books, including the 127-page paperback called *Stand up and be Counted*. I have already referred to it several times, but now we look briefly at how the invitation system was re-instituted at Westminster Chapel. Dr Campbell Morgan, the predecessor to Dr Martyn Lloyd Jones, used to employ the method.

In the introduction R. T. Kendall describes how Arthur Blessitt made an invitation at the close of his address at Westminster Chapel, which the author claims changed the whole history of that illustrious church in the heart of London. Blessitt broke the ice and now R. T. Kendall claims that warmer waters have been swum in ever since. It is no secret that some leading church officers and members would say 'murkier waters' would be a better description than 'warmer waters'. R. T. Kendall points to the recommendation by Luis Palau that the appeal system should be used regularly in our churches, perhaps once a month, without waiting for a special mission. Dr Kendall then says that he prefers the title 'public pledge' for the system of calling people forward at the close of an evangelistic sermon. The rest of the book consists of a polemic – historical, biblical and practical – in favour of the public pledge.

At this point, it will be helpful to recall the repudiation both by Billy Graham and Luis Palau that conversion is connected to the mechanics of moving to the front at the end of a service. This is a crucial issue and I therefore quote R. T. Kendall verbatim: 'But what I have been careful *not* to say is that the act of walking forward is *receiving* Christ. The primary purpose of the public pledge is to *confess* Christ; the instrumental purpose is to *seek* the Lord.'[13]

Dr Kendall places the emphasis on courage and devotes a chapter of his book to that attribute, with telling anecdotes to drive the point home. Also, he relates how Josif Ton, a very well-known evangelical leader from Oradea, Romania, now living in America, was a major influence in persuading him to use the invitation system at Westminster Chapel. For pastoral reasons, Josif Ton believes that in his country, which is controlled by Communists, it is important for those who profess the faith to be courageous and break with the bondage of fear. Often Communist informers are present at meetings. Dr Kendall describes in detail the method he has developed. It is different from that of Billy Graham or Luis Palau. He prays a brief and slow prayer, which possible penitents can easily follow, at the end of the service. Then, while the closing hymn is sung, he gives the opportunity for those who have prayed that prayer sincerely in their hearts to come forward and confess their faith. Doing this, he claims, is a signal to the rest of the world for that person that he or she has received Christ and constitutes an open profession of faith. Sometimes Dr Kendall will make an appeal for genuine backsliders to come forward. He says he exercises great care not to draw forward the 'overly scrupulous', who are not backsliders, but who merely have sensitive consciences.

Conclusion

We have now traversed several centuries, giving more detailed attention to our modern epoch. We have considered present-day leading evangelists and referred to the call that is going out from a famous London church in the shadow of Buckingham Palace — a call for the invitation system to be used in all the evangelical churches.

It is noteworthy that these leaders feel it is necessary to clear themselves of the charge of decisional regeneration. The reason for this is that the concept that regeneration is dependent upon the human will and that concession of the will to Christ is *the* crucial issue. Most professing Christians do not read books which expound these issues and in their minds the new birth follows a decision. Even though there are disclaimers, the machinery of crusade evangelism, with its emphasis on the invitation system and the use of the 'appeal' in churches, serves to fuel the concept of decisional regeneration to the point where it is in danger of becoming what I call a new evangelical sacrament.

Footnotes

1. *The Effective Invitation*, p. 83.
2. As above, p. 84.
3. As above, p. 89.
4. *Stand up and be Counted*, p. 46.
5. As above, p. 48.
6. *The Effective Invitation*, p. 94ff.
7. Winthrop S. Hudson, *Religion in America*, N.Y., 1973, p. 142.
8. J. F. Thornbury, *God Sent Revival*, E.P., p. 160ff.
9. Sydney E. Ahlstrom, *A Religious History of the American People*, Yale University Press, 1972, p. 460.
10. cf *God Sent Revival.* Chapter 33 provides an excellent discussion of this theme.
11. *The Effective Invitation*, p. 102.
12. As above, p. 119ff. Iain Murray's booklet, *The Invitation System*, is published by the Banner of Truth.
13. *Stand up and be Counted*, p. 83.

7.
A new evangelical sacrament?

The question mark to the title of this chapter is very important. I am not saying that the organized invitation system or
'appeal' practice as a whole is used in the way which will
be explained. I am asking the question: does it not lead to
that? Also has the practice not led to that in some quarters,
as is documented in the preface? As explained in chapter 1,
the 'appeal' is used in many different forms. Mostly it is
employed in a traditional way or cultural manner. Like
many other terms, the word 'sacrament' can be understood
in a good and a bad sense. I will show historically how it
has come to be used and will apply that usage to our subject.

It is a pity that while many are careful and seek to guard
against abuse others are not. Certainly the cautions of
R. Alan Streett in his book *The Effective Invitation* are
wholly inadequate and the trend and direction of that
presentation is towards a new evangelical sacrament. Going
forward or being an enquirer is easily regarded or viewed as
being saved or converted.[1]

What is a sacrament?

The word 'sacrament' is not in the Bible. Its meaning has to
be determined by the way in which it has developed in the
history of the church. The early pastors of the primitive
church divided their congregations into three distinct classes:
the heathen enquirers, the catachumens and the communi-
cants. After a service with prayer, singing and preaching, the
heathen section of the congregation was dismissed with the

104

formula: *'Ite, missa est!'* ('Go, it is dismissed!') Then the catachumens or candidates for baptism were instructed. They in turn were dismissed with the identical formula: *'Ite, missa est!'* Now only the highest class or part of the congregation remained. Together they celebrated the Lord's Supper. This was regarded as a sacred rite. Not one of the uninitiated was allowed to see it.

The Grecian background of those times assisted the notion of mysteriousness or mystery when it came to the uninitiated being kept out. The reason for this was that the religious Grecian sects had their own rites, rather like the Masons of our day. These rites could not possibly be discovered by the outsiders, the uninitiated.

The Lord's Supper came to be regarded as an innermost secret for those initiated, while the repetitive formula *'Ite, missa est!'* provided the word 'mass'. The word 'sacrament' comes from the Latin *'sacramentum'*, which means an oath and which was used by soldiers swearing allegiance to Rome or to Caesar. Baptism and the Lord's Supper were regarded as sacred rites or seals binding the partakers as by oath.

Gradually there developed the acceptance of seven sacraments: baptism, confirmation, the Lord's Supper, penance, marriage, orders and extreme unction. Of these baptism and the Lord's Supper have always been regarded as supreme. A further development of great moment was the notion that actual spiritual power is contained in the sacraments. Particularly is this the case with baptism and the Lord's Supper.

In the case of baptism the candidate is supposed to be born again or regenerated as the formula is spoken and as the baptismal water is applied. Likewise, in the mass when the bell sounds and the Host is elevated transubstantiation takes place. Mysteriously and miraculously the bread is supposed to turn into the literal flesh of Christ. Mysteriously, too, virtue is supposed to be received by those who take the 'Host' or wafer in the mass.

We should observe the subtle way in which great spiritual power is assumed by those who claim the right to dispense these sacraments. If the miracle of regeneration is brought about by a ritual controlled by man, then those who administer the rite claim to have salvation in their hands. Likewise in the administration of the mass the church that dispenses it and the priests who administer it claim power which is virtually miraculous power or the power of God himself.

Having provided the background concerning sacraments, I will now comment in particular on the mass. There are a number of features regarding this sacrament which can be compared with and which resemble the features surrounding the public appeal.

The first feature to note about the mass is the human control of miraculous power. The ritual is something entirely in the control of men. A second feature is the mystery surrounding the mass, while a third feature is the elaborate detail which characterizes the ceremony for the mass. A fourth feature is the centrality of this particular sacrament. A book has recently been published, which consists of the sayings by the present pope, John Paul II, concerning the Eucharist for mass. To him and to the Roman church it is the centre piece of Christianity. This is what Pope John Paul II declares: 'The Eucharist is also the centre of the Church's unity, as well as her greatest treasure. In the words of the Second Vatican Council, the Eucharist contains "the Church's entire spiritual wealth" ' (*Presbytyterorum Ordinis,* 5).'[2]

A fifth feature should be noted, which is that those who disregard the mass are viewed with displeasure. A Roman Catholic edict or canon was issued in 1982 to the effect that Protestants who partake of the mass must first signify their agreement with the transubstantiation which it signifies. In the history of the Reformation and the subsequent outcome many gave their lives in martyrdom rather than submit to the doctrine of transubstantiation.

Having outlined the features of the mass, I will now compare these with the 'appeal' as it has developed and as it is practised in some areas. I emphasize *some* areas — *not all!*

The most prominent feature of the invitation system is that the power of God is embraced within it. When the sinner responds then that is the basis of the miracle of the new birth. A second feature is the mystery which has developed concerning the sacred moments of decision or response. The impression given is that everything in the meeting is to be built up to this moment of human response. While great importance is placed on responding to the appeal, there is also the prominence of the enquiry room and what takes place there afterwards. In his book Streett relates the example of John Dillinger, a man who became a notorious criminal. As a boy Dillinger went forward to the altar rail. No one went to pray with him. In just a few minutes he walked to the back of the church and said to his sister, 'I'm never going into another church again!'[3] Streett laments this as though everything depended on the method used. He is consistent within the framework of his teaching, which is that everything depends on how the sinner is impressed. Needless to say, terrible bondage can come to us if we believe that so much depends upon a method or technique. It does not seem to enter Streett's mind that true repentance involves a settled determination to seek God with all one's heart until he is found. If the young Dillinger was a subject of the Holy Spirit's work he would not only seek God for a few minutes, but not stop seeking him over weeks or months or years — if necessary, all his life.

To continue with our observation of the features which characterize the invitation system, we note that elaborate detail often comes to surround the administration of the call for response. Even though Scripture is silent about this matter, evangelists devote detailed attention to the actual procedures or forms which they use. This extends to musical accompaniment and the place of persuasive hymns. Even the question of lighting and its effects has sometimes been considered and brought into operation.

A fourth feature similar to that of the mass is the centrality of the 'appeal' in modern evangelism. Success or failure is measured in terms of the numbers who respond. It is not difficult to imagine the pressure placed upon preachers to induce results. In some instances this has led to an observation on the humorous side because the matter can become ludicrous. It is said in some churches that if the preacher is unable to get people to come to the front then the call should be made for all men who love their mothers to respond and show their love by coming forward! If a man's mother was present, how could he possibly refuse such a call to go forward?

A fifth observation concerns the insistence on using the invitation system. Recently a personal friend of mine was called to a church in America on condition that he maintained the 'altar call' method. He does not believe in the system at all and has somehow to come to terms with this by the way he employs it.

Not all these features that I have referred to will apply in all instances, but we should be able to see the parallel with the mass. Needless to say, the mass is a human invention and is described as 'a fable' in Article 31 of the Thirty-Nine Articles of the Church of England. We should note that the success of a preacher will be measured in the great Day of Judgement according to the enduring effects of his ministry upon his hearers and according to how they have been built up in their faith.

Billy Graham, Luis Palau and R. T. Kendall might express their reservations concerning the act of response being equal to the new birth, but to those who observe the system the visible response is taken as salvation. The majority of evangelicals would not construe all those who go forward as being saved, but many do have an exaggerated view of the results. Thus prominently expressed in Kendall's book *Stand up and be Counted* is the astounding claim of 200,000 converts in the United Kingdom for Billy Graham! That is an incredible statistic. In the largest and most intense crusade, that at Harringay, which is regarded as by far the most successful, there were 36,431 inquirers. Ernest Reisinger in his book *Today's Evangelism* declares of the invitation system: 'This unbiblical system has produced the greatest record of false statistics ever compiled by church or business.'[4]

At the time of the Reformation there were those who were cynical about the erroneous practices of the church. There were also those who abused the system. One such was Johann Tetzel (1465—1519), a German Dominican preacher who was appointed Inquisitor for Poland in 1509. He used the sacramental superstition to the point where it was claimed that souls were released from purgatory by generous donations being given to the church. Even the timing of the release was advertised by Tetzel, who said that at the very moment when the coins hit the bottom of the box, a poor soul suffering in the fires of purgatory would be released. We have our extremists today who use the 'appeal' in a sacramental way. I recall a conversation in America in which a pastor's wife narrated to me her experience as a counsellor. In counselling someone who came forward she discovered that this enquirer had no concept of repentance or faith. She endeavoured therefore to explain the gospel in a simple manner. The leader of the meeting in the meantime began to be impatient and after about ten minutes could stand it no longer. Sweeping the woman counsellor aside, he took over as follows:

'You don't want to go to hell, do you?'

'No!'

'You do want to go to heaven, don't you?'

'Yes, I do!'

'You believe that Christ died for sinners, don't you?'

'Yes, I do!'

'Then let's give thanks that he died for you and has given you salvation.'

Then the leader prayed as follows: 'Lord I thank you for giving this soul eternal life. Thank you, Lord, Amen.'

Then, turning to the person in question, he said, 'Now you have eternal life and you can praise the Lord! Go and tell your friends that you have been saved!'

When methods like these come to predominate in a variety of quarters then we must say that a new evangelical sacrament has appeared on the stage of modern-day evangelical Christianity.

Footnotes
1. For examples see *The Effective Invitation*, pp. 50 and 184.
2. Pope John Paul II, *The Bread of Life*, St Paul Publications, p. 56.
3. *The Effective Invitation*, p. 182.
4. Ernest Reisinger, *Today's Evangelism*, Presbyterian and Reformed, p. 76.

8.
The 'appeal' examined in the light of Scripture

We have established that there is no contention whatever about the rightness of calling on men everywhere to repent, to believe and to come to Christ and trust him for personal salvation. There is no dispute about the urgency of the gospel, or about the fact that justification and new life are immediate when a soul is joined to Christ by faith. There is no disagreement about the necessity of seeking to make disciples of all men, which includes seeking to persuade men to conform in every way to our Lord Jesus Christ and all his commandments. Nor is there any difference of opinion about the necessity of making baptism the goal, according to the Great Commission of Matthew 28:18–20. When disciples are made and so taught that they understand and believe in the Trinity and have a credible evidence of repentance towards God and faith in our Lord Jesus Christ, they ought to be baptized.

It is also clear that there should be liberty and flexibility in dealing with any unusual situation in which revival may break out and it may be necessary to gather people together for counselling and for further instruction, arranging to meet them and making time to guide them as certainly as we can to assurance of salvation in our Saviour. I am not saying that it is inappropriate for any preacher or minister to use his common sense in handling a situation in which there is concern or distress and there is a paramount need for people to receive help and biblical directions.

We are, however, in contention about whether there is a fixed policy and a standard practice which *has* to be used for calling people to the front. My contention is that there is no evidence at all to suggest that a standard form or practice was ever devised, suggested or practised either in the Old or the New Testament. Furthermore, the practice cannot be warranted by inference from any biblical passages.

Streett, however, argues as follows: 'The first-century gospel preacher always concluded his evangelistic sermon with an appeal for the unconverted present to repent of their sins and place their faith in the crucified and resurrected Lord of Glory. Often these appeals called upon the individuals additionally to demonstrate their sincerity by taking a public stand for Christ before friends, relatives, neighbours, and even enemies. This call for the sinner or new convert to make an initial public confession of faith is the basis for the modern-day practice of extending a public invitation.

'Two types of public invitation were used in the New Testament times. The first called for sinners to demonstrate publicly their desire to repent and believe, and was used as a means of bringing them to a state of conversion.

'The second called upon new converts, who had been supernaturally transformed by the message, openly to witness to their newfound faith.'[1]

Now if we examine the first paragraph above we should note the statement: 'These appeals called upon the individuals additionally to demonstrate their sincerity by taking a public stand for Christ before friends, relatives, neighbours, and even enemies.' When we search the New Testament we cannot find any reference or evidence of a special call to the front by way of appeal. If no New Testament evidence may be found for this, we must come to the conclusion that Streett reached an erroneous conclusion in saying that the basis for modern-day practice of extending a public invitation is based upon the examples of the New Testament.

When we look at the second paragraph we see that Streett is maintaining that the first kind of appeal was for people publicly to demonstrate their repentance and faith and that it was actually employed as a means of 'bringing them to a state of conversion'. Here we have the basis of what I have called 'the new evangelical sacrament'. Here we have the actual point at which converts are manufactured by the art of getting them to respond in a typical fashion of coming forward. No matter how ardently it is denied that this actually brings regeneration, it is inferred and is very widely assumed in the evangelical circles where it is practised.

When we examine the third paragraph of Streett's statement we have no problem with it if he is referring to the New Testament teaching that people should be publicly baptized. We ought to observe, however, that it is not possible to read into the accounts that are given of the baptisms that they were specially to be made public events. Certainly John the Baptist baptized out in the open and we can hardly imagine that the baptisms at Pentecost were not public, but this is not always the case and nor is there any stress or command that it should be so. The Philippian jailer was baptized at night in a prison and the Ethiopian eunuch in the desert. I am not contending about this particular matter and personally enjoy baptismal services with as many people from the public present as possible. What I am saying is that the matter is open-ended in the New Testament, which is just as well, because in times of persecution it has not always been expedient to expose converts immediately to the wrath of the enemies of the gospel by deliberately thrusting them into the public gaze. But now, with our Bibles open, let us search for any kind of basic accepted procedure at the end of meetings for people to come forward by way of a public response.

Both Matthew and Mark record times of extended preaching to vast crowds of people — teaching which lasted two, three or four days. There are the two instances of crowds of approximately twenty thousand and then possibly sixteen thousand who stayed so long and were so involved in hearing our Lord that a difficult situation arose with regard to their being able to make their homeward journey without fainting with hunger. In both cases we have the record of the miracle of the multiplying of the loaves and fish.

Now, with a superb opportunity of being able to gather as many as possible into the gospel net, why is it that there is no record of our Lord attempting to get people to make a public profession? On the contrary, when we read John's account there is an emphasis on the unbelief of the people and also of many disciples deserting Jesus in spite of his miraculous powers. Further investigation reveals that the people were offended by his preaching. Nor did our Lord try to remove this offence. He did not seek to make himself as popular as possible and by this means to win the favour of the people.

It might be argued that our Lord's purpose was to prepare for his passion and this was the reason why there is no record of a concerted effort made by him to gather in souls. However, this argument is not satisfactory because in the same context and at the same time our Lord was sending out his disciples to preach the gospel in all the towns and villages to which he himself was intending to come.

Furthermore, when we move to the book of Acts, we find that Peter did not try to endear himself to the people and nor did he make any appeal at Pentecost for people to come forward. His purpose was to bring them to a conviction of sin for their terrible guilt of participating in the death of Christ. When the Holy Spirit came upon these proselytes, whose practice it was to study the Scriptures, their conviction was very deep. As I sought to demonstrate in chapter 6, we have in Pentecost a fulfilment of Zechariah 12:10–14. The repentance was of a grief-stricken kind. This needs to be asserted because many make the mistake of thinking that people can be rushed to baptism on the grounds that the procedure was so swift at the time of Pentecost. We must remember that those converts represented the cream of the Old Testament believers, who travelled hundreds of miles to spend a protracted time of religious observance and study in the city of Jerusalem.

The intensity of devotion and the sincerity and depth of the converts is shown by their steadfastness in continuing in the teaching after their baptism and in their observation of the ordinances of the Lord, not to mention their devotion in selling their possessions and goods and sharing them with anyone who had need (Acts 2:42–47; 4:32–35). They were obviously free to meet every day, which might suggest that time had been set apart for religious conference away from the normal secular demands of life.

When we move on through the book of Acts, we find that it is quite incorrect to suggest that a special form of

appeal was used by the apostles. The opposite seems to be
the case. A full report is given of Paul and Barnabas in
Pisidian Antioch, where Paul terminated his address with
a most scathing warning. He then promptly left the
synagogue. It was an exciting time because the Gentiles
flocked in large numbers to hear Paul and Barnabas and
this would have seemed the perfect moment for the Holy
Spirit to introduce the practice of the 'appeal' or invitation
system — but no, all it says is that the Gentiles 'were glad
and honoured the word of the Lord; and all who were
appointed for eternal life believed'! (Acts 13:48.)

When we come to the much-debated sermon by Paul
preached at Athens, we discover that no appeal was made
by him at all. Indeed, he simply terminated the meeting
and all we are told is 'A few men became followers of
Paul and believed.' It is not necessary to make a public
appeal in order to gather those who are interested. One
has simply to intimate either in the address or to some
present that you would like to continue to discourse with
a smaller group afterwards, and it is plain that there were
just a few who desired to talk further with Paul. A prominent person by the name of Dionysius was one of these,
as well as a woman named Damaris.

As we read through Acts, we discover that instead of
statistics being reported of people coming forward for
counselling or for baptism, we read rather of those who
became obstinate and who refused to believe (Acts 19:9).
This reporting of opposition and difficulty is very important because it accords very much with the reality of what
is involved in promulgating the gospel in an unbelieving
world.

The book of Acts ends with an account of Paul being
able to give hospitality, albeit restricted because of his
captivity, to all who wanted to come and see him. This
is an encouraging note on which to conclude because it
reminds us that quality in the Lord's work is based upon
personal relationships. The question which must really
be examined is whether it is wise for people to be counselled by complete strangers. In unusual circumstances
this may be necessary, but the preferable procedure is
always that we foster personal relationships of trust and

fellowship. The wonderful account of Philemon and also the details provided concerning Epaphroditus (Phil. 2:19—30) illustrate that Paul was never an evangelist in the distance, but one who personally identified with and helped the personal spiritual needs of individuals. This brings us directly and logically to the example of our Lord in dealing with individuals.

The rich young man who came with such eagerness to Jesus to enquire after eternal life for himself is an outstanding example of individual counselling. Far from seeking to bring the young man to an immediate decision, our Lord posed to him the great exacting issues of the law and personal commitment and spelt out in a very graphic way the cost of discipleship. The young man revealed by his attitude that he did not understand the nature of sin and certainly had not come to terms with the cost of discipleship. He went away deeply troubled. We are left without a knowledge of what ultimately happened in his soul, or whether he came to a different mind through the Holy Spirit using the truths that our Lord had brought to his attention.

This example is important because it shows that there ought always to be a two-way traffic in our preaching. The modern decisionist methods represent a one-way traffic of only aiming at people coming forward, whereas the biblical teaching frequently reveals that people ought to be sent in the other direction as well.

It is fascinating and worthwhile to make a comparison of the different ways in which our Lord dealt with a variety of individuals. For instance, we can compare the seemingly harsh approach that he employed with the Syrophenician woman (Mark 7:24—30) with the instant calling of Zacchaeus (Luke 19:5—7). Streett makes much of the fact that Zacchaeus was called down from his sycamore fig tree *in public*, but it is hard to see how there was any other way! To show that it was not a matter of stressing the public side of things, we can compare the cases of the healing of a deaf and dumb man. Our Lord was careful to take him aside away from the crowd (Mark 7:31—36). Likewise in the healing of a blind man, our Lord took him by the hand and led him outside the village away from everybody in order to deal with him (Mark 8:22—26).

Before we turn to the Old Testament, reference should be made to Streett's claim that the word *'parakaleo'* in the Greek can be translated as 'give an invitation'. On this basis he reads into Acts 2:38–41 that Peter 'called for his listeners to respond publicly to his message by presenting themselves to him'. What are we to say to this claim? The answer is that the term 'to call' used in crucial passages like Romans 8:30, 2 Timothy 1:9 and 2 Peter 1:10, tells of the sovereign call of God the Father. These passages emphasize that calling and election go together. The way in which the verb is used in Acts 2:39 stresses not only the sovereignty of God, but adoption. The calling is *to* the Father, to be with him or alongside of him.

The conclusion is that we can never do this calling ourselves. Only the Father can do it. It is imperative that he do it through the appointed means, as he did at Pentecost — namely preaching. We are not calling people or inviting them to stand alongside ourselves. The Father sovereignly calls his elect. He does this in an infallible way. If we attempt to do it and issue an invitation by which we persuade twenty people to come to the front, are we going to say that our call approximates to the sovereign call of God the Father? It is true that the word *'parakaleo'* is used to convey different meanings, such as 'to comfort' (Matt. 2:18), or 'to plead with' or 'beseech' (Matt. 8:5; Acts 19:31), or 'to request' or 'exhort' (Acts 14:22), but it is certainly stretching the use of this word to try and make it vindicate a call to the front, especially when no examples of this can be found in the New Testament.

An examination of the Old Testament

The favourite references used by those wishing to uphold the public invitation system are three: the case of Moses reported in Exodus 32:19, 20, 26; Joshua as reported in Joshua 24:16, 24–27; and Elijah on Mount Carmel, 1 Kings 18:37–39. If we want to be thorough we might add the case of Josiah renewing the covenant reported in 2 Kings 23:1–3.

At the outset we should remember that in every one of these situations an entirely different set of circumstances existed and in each case the Holy Spirit gave directions which were unique to that situation.

What we have to fix firmly in our minds is that these were not Billy Graham Crusades. They were not Southern Baptist Revival meetings. Nor were they Billy Sunday campaigns, in which the objective was to get as many people to hit the sawdust trail as possible!

They were all entirely different situations and not a set of gatherings that can be collated in order to establish a pattern for modern 'appeal' methods. Let us remember that Joshua was dealing with a situation which involved establishing the loyalty of the subjects of the theocracy. Immediately after he had said, 'Choose for yourselves this day whom you will serve,' and then given the exhortation: 'But as for me and my household, we will serve the Lord,' the people answered that they would be faithful and serve the Lord. Joshua then denied their ability and said to them, 'You are not able to serve the Lord. He is a holy God; he is a jealous God. He will not forgive your rebellion and your sins.' Far from an appeal for people to come forward, we have here an Old Testament instance of a fierce denunciation of the depravity of the human heart and a stress on the need to recognize our own inabilities. This fosters dependence upon the Lord's grace towards us and warns us not to trust in ourselves or our best resolutions.

The situation with Moses was quite different because there was a desperate rebellion, almost like a civil war, which ended with a tremendous execution of rebels by the Levites. When Moses called for those who were on the Lord's side to come to him, he was not calling for decisions for Christ and for people to come forward to be counselled for salvation or to come down the aisles to enter the enquiry room to give their names and addresses. He was calling for those who would have the grim task of weeding out rebels and putting them to the sword.

I have mentioned Joshua before Moses because I wish to compare the circumstances just related with those of Elijah reported in 1 Kings 18:19—40. It was clear that Elijah's intention was to expose the evil and futile nature of Baal worship. At the conclusion of the dramatic proceedings Elijah commanded that all the prophets of Baal be seized and his express command was that not one of them should escape. They were all taken down to the Kishon Valley, where they were executed. It is easy to see that the actual physical execution of 450 false prophets is a very different kind of scene from that envisaged in an evangelistic campaign, when according to the inevitable procedure as many people as possible are urged to come to the front. There is no evidence that Elijah was gathering the people of Israel for spiritual counsel and nor is there any evidence that the people were spiritually dedicated or well taught. Indeed, by common consent it is believed by many commentators that it was because of the failure of the people to be turned in their hearts to God that Elijah suffered his deep depression. The demeanour of the Israelites would be one of national patriotism rather than one of spirituality. The circumstances certainly did not require an enquiry room for souls to be counselled concerning faith and repentance.

Another Old Testament reference which has been cited as an example of the invitation system is the story of King Josiah in 2 Kings 23:1–3. The scene is one of great encouragement because of the king's zeal for reformation and his example in dedicating himself to renewing the covenant in the presence of the Lord and the gathered community. As for the public response, we are told nothing about what they were asked to do or how indeed they actually evidenced the pledging of themselves to the coven-ant. If it was desirable for all the people to come forward and sign a book I would find nothing wrong with that. Nor would there be anything wrong with the people standing up or putting their hands up or all joining together to make some audible affirmation of faith. What I am stressing is that every situation is different and that this one is again very far removed from an evangelistic campaign, in which the great objective is to get people to move down the aisles at the end of a service to record their willingness to close with Christ. To illustrate the matter further, Josiah did not set up a regular evening meeting or a regular weekly meeting or even an annual meeting in which to establish an ordinance by which the people would have to pledge themselves. In our modern evangelical scene, as I have been at pains to show, many are coming into an absolute bondage concerning the matter of a set system for the 'appeal'.

Another Old Testament incident referred to as evidence for the invitation system is the public pledge related in Genesis 14. Here Abram said to the King of Sodom, 'I have raised my hand to the Lord, God Most High, Creator of heaven and earth, and have taken an oath that I will accept nothing belonging to you, not even a thread or the thong of a sandal, so that you will never be able to say, "I made Abram rich"' (Gen. 14:22, 23). From these verses Dr Kendall establishes ten points:

1. What Abraham said to the King of Sodom was a *pledge*.
2. It was public.
3. It was Abraham's *personal decision*.
4. It was a pledge not only before the world but *before God*.
5. The pledge shows that Abraham was not only unashamed of his testimony, but that he wanted to be *identified* with the true God: 'I have raised my hand to the Lord.'
6. Abraham obviously believed all that he affirmed in his *heart*.
7. There is no hint that Abraham thought he was righteous because he made this confession.
8. This pledge was made *immediately following* his encounter with Melchizedek — a 'type of Christ'.
9. As a pledge equally points to a commitment that goes beyond the present moment, Abraham vowed to the King of Sodom that he would take nothing.
10. Abraham's public pledge implies a separation from the world.[2]

In analysing Dr Kendall's thesis we need to see that precisely the same principle applies here as with all the other instances used from the Old Testament to try to establish a set order for an invitation system. That principle is that in every instance the historical background and circumstances are different. R. T. Kendall falls into the same trap as does Streett, because he reads far too much into this incident in the life of Abraham. From the text all that we can establish is that it was a purely straightforward declaration of intention by Abraham to the pagan king. There was no crowd involved nor was any great principle being established. The distance that has to be travelled from this isolated instance of a confrontation between two leaders and the whole ethos of our modern church meetings or evangelistic meetings is enormous. For instance, Abraham raising his hand as a token of his determination not to receive any material advantage from the King of Sodom has no connection whatever with people raising their hands in response to an evangelistic appeal.

Both Streett and R. T. Kendall use the calling of Adam and Eve from behind the bushes where they were hiding to try to establish the need to call people to the front. Here again we must say that a preacher is never God, even though he may speak as a prophet declaring the mind and will of God. The two things are not compatible by way of comparison.

My conclusion is that these writers are desperate to find scriptural evidences. R. T. Kendall uses Genesis 41:43 to make the point that courage in public is required by God. This incident tells of Pharaoh's courage in believing Joseph's words on the spot and 'putting his own honour and credibility on the line by publicly accepting the word of a Hebrew prisoner'. Now what Pharaoh, as a man of great power and authority does in an unusual and peculiar set of circumstances, is no basis for establishing the set principle which is urged upon all ministers by Dr Kendall to practise in their churches as a matter of course in their regular ministries.

Dr Kendall devotes a whole chapter to the necessity of courage. Coming forward at the conclusion of a meeting shows courage. It is hard to find courage in any of the lists of Christian attributes such as those given in Matthew 5, 2 Peter 1 or Colossians 3. The difficulty is that the naturally courageous might easily be led into presumption because of this factor in their temperament, while those who are reserved and withdrawing might easily find this a major stumbling-block and have a guilt complex sown within them. They might feel rejected and condemned because they could not pluck up the courage demanded by the preacher or the evangelist. The Scriptures make it clear that repentance towards God and faith in the Lord Jesus Christ are what is required, not the attribute of courage. It is not by *courage* we are saved, but by *faith*. As soon as we add dimensions of our own, we confuse the gospel. There will be many of sensitive and nervous disposition in heaven and many self-confident, naturally courageous people in hell.

Of all characters in the Bible John the Baptist can be regarded as one who called on people to make a public response. We cannot substantiate this with any detail, but there is a case for calling on people who are guilty of certain sins and requiring of them some evidence of their repentance. This cannot be done in private and if people have been offended by their behaviour or cruelty then it is fitting that there should be some public renunciation of the evils done. As we have noted already, the baptism of believers is the public act specified in the New Testament, not inviting people to the front. Baptism is greatly neglected in this whole debate because the famous evangelists do not have to concern themselves with it. I am persuaded that this is the key to correcting the confusion that has spread because of the 'appeal'. In the baptism of believers we are gathering those who have been taught and who have come by the new birth into union with the Father, the Son and the Holy Spirit, according to the terms of the Great Commission as expressed in Matthew 28:18–20. It is important that we understand the new birth and to that subject we now turn.

Footnotes
1. *The Effective Invitation*, p. 55.
2. *Stand up and be Counted,* p. 39 ff.

9.
A key issue - the new birth

The philosophy or system of calling for 'decisions' fails to comprehend the new birth at every point. It fails to see firstly, that the new birth is a new creation; secondly, that the new birth cannot come from the flesh; thirdly, that the new birth comes from God alone; fourthly, that there is a preparatory work to regeneration; and, finally, that the means employed to bring about the new birth is the truth. The chief means employed by God is preaching, not counselling techniques or manipulation of human emotions.

1. The new birth is a new creation

The new birth is described as a creation. If any person be in Christ he is a new creature or new creation (2 Cor. 5:17). This change involves a new heart or a new spirit. It is a universal change of the whole man. As a new creation it extends to every part of man — his understanding, will, conscience and affections.

As the whole man was corrupted by sin and made alien to God, now the whole person is made anew by the Spirit. Whereas the whole person in all his faculties was anti-God, now the whole person in all his faculties is pro-God. He now loves and obeys the triune God.

The word 'birth' in the expression 'new birth' is helpful because when a babe is formed in the womb all the parts of that child are formed together — not some parts and not others, for that would be disastrous. All parts are formed in proportion to each other.

In his great book *The Religious Affections* Jonathan Edwards insists on symmetry or proportion as an essential mark of a genuine work of God in the soul. Writing from the vantage-point of experience in revival, Edwards explained that even in a time of great religious awakening we must not rush to the conclusion that all who profess Christ are born again. There may be appearances of love, as well as zeal and praise and great fluency and fervour, but we should look for deeper marks than that. There must be pleasure in the holiness of God, humility and spiritual fruit in daily living. And then Edwards stresses the necessity of beautiful symmetry and proportion in the whole nature of a person.

Dr Martyn Lloyd-Jones in the fourteenth chapter of his book *Preaching and Preachers* gives nine reasons why he never employed the invitation system. All his reasons are related more or less to this subject of the new birth. The first reason, and probably the most telling, is that the emphasis on 'decisions' bypasses the mind and affections of a man and aims directly at his will. The doctor reminds us of Romans 6:17, where the apostle says, 'God be thanked that ye were the servants of sin, but ye have obeyed from the heart that form of doctrine which was delivered you' (AV). Obedience is required from the heart. How can we expect obedience to all that the gospel requires if there is not a new heart, if there has been no regeneration?

Most preachers know very well that we can use the truth of God backed with the power of our personality to persuade people to agree to put right various aspects of their lives. We can bring about restored family relationships, but how well we know from experience that unless God is in the heart of the matter, healing does not last!

In the same way, it is possible to persuade people to make decisions. This is especially easy with children. It is common to find young people who have gone forward several times. They have been through the process of believing and trusting many times, but it has not worked. As soon as they were back in difficult circumstances at school and at home, there was no spiritual reality in their lives. They are not born again and they know it. How do you counsel such people? And what is the response of those who call for decisions when confronted by people who have come forward and gone through the motions or the formula several times?

How easy it is to go direct to a person's emotions, elicit a decision through a prayer, or by the imposition of a prayer, but leave that person entirely unchanged! Directly to assault the will or emotions but to bypass the mind is equally dangerous as new birth involves a re-creation of the mind as well as the heart.

2. The new birth cannot come from the flesh

Our Lord at one and the same time asserted the necessity of the new birth and also its authorship: it is not from the flesh; it is from the Spirit. From a doctrinal point of view a study of Romans convinced me of the error of pressing for decisions in the mechanical manner we have been discussing. The case against it was proved by the time I had reached the end of chapter 3. I came to see the futility of expecting the new birth to come from the flesh. Especially convincing were the words of Paul: 'There is no one who seeks God' (Rom. 3:11). The new birth must come from God alone, and in order to do that he had to work in people to make them willing to listen and be taught. That is something which we examined in detail in chapter 5 under the subject of preparationism.

There is no spiritual spark, no power, no source of generation whatsoever in a corrupt sinner that contributes to his new birth. Nor are we ever given to understand that the Holy Spirit puts a spiritual battery charger into the dead sinner and says, 'There you are, now I have given you free will, use the battery charger, and when you do I will come into you and give you the new birth, which is a total change of your whole nature.' Nor are we to believe that the Holy Spirit asks permission of dead corrupt sinners to come and regenerate them, no more than he will ask permission to raise the dead out of their graves in that great day when the trumpet will sound (1 Cor. 15:52). He does not ask if they are willing. They are not willing! He makes them willing in the day of his power (Ps. 110:3, AV). Only someone with a new heart and a new spirit is willing (Ezek.

36:26). The carnal nature will never be willing for it is at enmity with God and is not subject to the law of God, neither indeed can be (Rom. 8:7, 8).

It should be clear from John 1:12, 13 that it is not possible to expect the new birth from a human decision. The text reads: 'Yet to all who received him, to those who believed in his name, he gave the right to become children of God — children born not of natural descent, nor of human decision or a husband's will, but born of God.' Parents would love to be able to regenerate their children and relatives. Can we do it by getting them to make a decision? Countless parents have tried this method and had their children record a decision, or several decisions, at special meetings, only to be disappointed by seeing no change. There is no way we can create their regeneration. There is much that we must and can do for their spiritual good, but we simply cannot create a new heart in them.

Nor does the power of the new birth lie in the Scripture *per se,* that is, by and in itself alone. God uses Scripture in bringing the new birth (James 1:18; 1 Peter 1:22). We often see young people wearing headphones connected to small cassette machines. If we recorded a cassette full of commands from Scripture and captured young people, bound them hand and foot, fixed the earphones on them and played the recordings, all our quotations would not give them new birth. Softly or loudly, by thunder or by sweet music, there is no conceivable way that man can induce the new birth. The Spirit sovereignly blows where and when he wills.

To emphasize the point, a friend of mine, who is a pastor in London, experienced the usual pattern of gradual growth in his church of about 150. Suddenly and unexpectedly twenty people in one week were lastingly saved. An observer said it was an example of sheer vertical sovereignty. I know another pastor friend who saw fourteen lastingly converted through one sermon. Needless to say, these men are only interested in what I have called 'lastingly'. They are hostile to the invitation system for the reasons I am explaining.

3. The new birth comes from God alone and in his time

We have just seen that the flesh cannot produce regeneration. What a glorious word was that which came to Ezekiel: 'I will make breath enter you, and you will come to life'! God alone is the author of creation. We who believe have been created in Christ Jesus (Eph. 2:10) and we are called new creations (Col. 3:10; 2 Cor. 5:17). The greatness of the act is seen in the power required to give us spiritual birth, which is described by Paul as 'an incomparably great power' (Eph. 1:19, 20). It is declared to be an exercise of divine power fully equal to that employed in raising Christ from the dead. Such a power belongs to God alone.

God's work in souls is likened to planting. Through Isaiah we have these words: 'They are the shoot I have planted, the work of my hands' (Isa. 60:21). And in the same context of divine planting versus human planting Christ warned, 'Every plant that my heavenly Father has not planted will be pulled up by the roots' (Matt. 15:13).

In his book Streett tells of an incident in the life of D. L. Moody which Moody regarded as the greatest blunder in his ministry. This was when he did not call for an immediate commitment but gave the congregation a week to think about it. At that very time the great fire of Chicago broke out and hundreds died in the city that week.

Not for one moment do I dispute that redemption is the most urgent matter in the world and that today is the day of salvation (2 Cor. 6:2). Also, it would be a strange preacher of eternal life and eternal damnation who did not have a sense of failure. The apostle Paul asked, 'Who is sufficient for these things?' The wonder of it is how Moody survived at all if he believed, as Streett implies that he did, that everything hinged on the methods he used. Because he failed to use the right method, that is, the invitation, those people were lost for eternity! On this basis we might as well change the wording of the Great Commission and say that it should read: 'Go and give invitations to all men and tell them that eternity hangs on their immediate response to your invitations and make sure you get the method right because they will be lost if you do not.' Rather the emphasis in the Great Commission is on teaching. So teach them that they will be ready for baptism into the Trinity.

Not only is the new birth a sovereign act of God, but the timing is according to his sovereign will too. As the wind is entirely beyond human control, so the Holy Spirit of God moves entirely according to his own timing. As no man can ever say that he is the author of his own natural birth, so no man can ever say that he is the author of his spiritual birth. The timing is of the Holy Spirit's will and purpose alone.

4. God prepares people for the new birth

What missionary agency advocating the appeal system today would tolerate William Carey taking eight years to secure the first convert? What agency that counts decisions would go on supporting a stalwart pioneer like James Haldane of Morocco, who laboured for forty years without a convert? How do we explain that people in darkness do not instantly respond to the gospel? There is a work of preparation in the souls of men before the new birth. As with the new birth, that work is the work of the Holy Spirit. We are to teach to the utmost of our ability.

There are those who advance considerably in knowledge and understanding before they are born again. We can deduce from passages like Hebrews 6:4—6 and 10:26—31 and 2 Peter 2:20 that it is possible for a person to advance far along the road of Christianity and yet be reprobate. We are certain that in order for a person to believe in the three persons of the Trinity he has to be taught substantially. I have explained the subject of preparation in chapter 5 where we saw that illumination or knowledge is not the only preliminary to the new birth. There is conviction of sin. This aspect of the gospel seems to have been forgotten today. In revivals people have been known to experience very intense convictions and yet afterwards fall away from those convictions and abandon the gospel. No degree of conviction is specified, but the promise Jesus made was that the Holy Spirit would convince the world of sin, righteousness and judgement. There must be some conviction of sin if a sinner is pleading for the forgiveness of sin. Sometimes convictions increase and then subside and then come on again before the new birth.

Yet another aspect of preparation is reformation. In almost every case of conversion I have witnessed in my own ministry, I have observed an improved attention to the means of grace prior to conversion, especially in listening to preaching. Sometimes this process has gone on for six months, sometimes a year, sometimes more. Of course, this does not apply to sudden conversions. One man I know, who had no background in Christian teaching, bought a *Reader's Digest* in order to enjoy a good lie-in on Sunday morning. He awoke and began to read. Strangely, he read of a Baptist church and wondered what that was, because he had seen a notice-board nearby with that name. Curiosity caused him to get dressed and investigate. He attended the morning service and returned again in the evening. God moved powerfully in his soul and by the evening he was a fervent believer, from which position he has never subsequently moved. We can all tell of such accounts, but they form the minority.

This principle of God moving in his own time occurs over and over again within crusade evangelism in defying all the mechanics of decision-making. One lady told me recently that after making a decision in a Pentecostal church she soon fell away because she received no substantial teaching. She became a Jehovah's Witness for twenty years. Then she experienced conviction of sin and attended a Luis Palau campaign for five nights in a row. The preaching was what she needed to bring her back to the point where she had been many years before. I urged her to make doubly sure that she continue to abide in Christ by doing what he commanded, that is to abide in his Word.

Just when is a person born again? How can we know the moment? Some Christians feel sure they know. They may be right, but only the Holy Spirit himself knows his own work. The new birth cannot be created by pressing for a decision. In teaching the inability of man in John 3 Jesus was bringing Nicodemus to see that he was not to rely on his own merits, but only on God. In the context of the famous John 3 passage the direction we are all pointed to is that of faith. We do have a work to do. We are to believe in God's sent Son (John 6:29). When a sinner does believe, it is not the meritorious cause of his salvation, only the instrumental cause. The timing of God's great creative act of regeneration belongs to him alone.

5. Preaching is the instrument of the new birth, not counselling techniques or manipulation of human emotions

Preaching holds the prime position as the means used by God in extending the kingdom of Christ and building up the church. 'God was pleased through the foolishness of what was preached to save those who believe' (1 Cor. 1:21). It is not by human wisdom, or by signs and miracles, but by preaching that God calls his people. 'Jews demand miraculous signs and Greeks look for wisdom, but we preach Christ crucified' (1 Cor. 1:22, 23).

It has never been easy to maintain the primacy of preaching. Today, more than ever, conditions around us militate against preaching. John Stott analyses various ways in which preaching has suffered as a means of grace. He discusses the influences which have had an adverse effect on the minds of people in their regard for gospel preaching. For instance, he elaborates on the banal effects of television and points to increasing physical laziness and intellectual flabbiness that result from excessive television viewing.[2]

When we relate this to preaching, we can ask the question, how we can expect people conditioned by sixteen to eighteen hours of TV a week to sit still and listen to one person talking without the aid of frills and light relief? This whole question is not unrelated to our subject, because a mentality has developed in which there is a great stress on entertainment and drama. We expect to be entertained and expect our thinking to be done for us. Through modern advertising we are saturated with the idea that we can obtain our needs quickly and easily. All these factors are related to evangelism in which the entertainment factor is now prominent. Having imbibed the values of the world, we also expect that there will be substantial, instant and plentiful results in our evangelistic campaigns.

All this bypasses the hard graft that is involved in teaching and preaching. A great work of persuasion by means of preaching precedes conversion. At least in most cases that is true. Yet today 'appeals' are made at gospel rock concerts where the preaching content is almost non-existent. That is an extreme example, but even in the case of the best gospel-preaching evangelists the emphasis on the invitation is so prominent and the focus on the counselling and the results so much to the fore that the preaching sinks into the background, almost as a subsidiary.

This whole ethos and emphasis of entertainment beforehand, especially conditioning by music and stress on the call to the front, favours well the theology of modern evangelicalism, which is that salvation stems from man's response, rather than God's election. An understanding of the significance of the new birth is designed to correct our practices and restore the concept that God's calling comes through powerful biblical preaching and that he will do all his calling by this means without the support of the call to the front.

At this point it will be helpful to answer questions that always lurk in our minds. Why should there be this emphasis on preaching? Why do the Scriptures insist on this, as we have seen from 1 Corinthians 1:20−25?

The answer surely is that the truth is the indispensable instrument by which an unregenerate mind is laid hold of and changed. The Holy Spirit takes the truth and applies it to the mind and heart of the hearer. In this way the person is turned inside out. Says James, 'He chose to give us birth through the word of truth' (James 1:18). The word as preached is the instrument, as Peter declares: 'For you have been born again, not of perishable seed, but of imperishable, through the living and enduring word of God' (1 Peter 1:23). It is not by a technique of bringing a person to say a prayer or make a decision that the new birth takes place. The new birth can never be brought about by manipulation.

This is not to say that the Holy Spirit does not use the Word in many different ways, such as through reading or personal witness. He is sovereign in using the means he chooses and coming at the time of his own choice. This in no way absolves us from the exacting work of preaching the gospel to all men and aiming at that quality of preaching which is effective. This is important because the employment of this means magnifies the author of salvation. It points vividly to the source of the new birth. James' statement highlights the will of the Father: 'Of his own will begat he us with the word of truth' (AV). The new birth is not due to any merit in us or the result of a response by us. Any true response by us or closing with Christ by us is predated or worked in us prior to the action. By the Father's omnipotence we are drawn (John 6:44).

We should not be surprised by this method. By employment of his word Jahweh spoke the universe into being. This way highlights his role as Creator and Author of all things. Likewise it was when he spoke to the patriarchs and prophets that the whole drama of redemption moved forward. Because he speaks it fixes our minds on the fact that he is the source, the stem and the origin of revelation and salvation. He did not consult with us about creation or about the unfolding of the history of redemption. Every move is a big surprise. For instance, suddenly he calls Abraham and suddenly he appears to Moses in the burning bush. All the way through we see the sovereign Lord as the prime mover, the originator and first cause. He commands and it is done. That too is the pattern in our calling.

When the emphasis is taken away from the preaching and centred on the 'appeal', then the stress is placed on the response of man as the all-important factor. This method is misleading because it places the new birth in a setting which ascribes it to man's power or will, when in fact it is the creation of God.

The new birth then, when rightly understood, concentrates our minds on the biblical means provided by God in the great and urgent work of evangelism. It points us to the primacy of preaching, however difficult that may be. We ought not to allow preaching to be usurped by other activities.

James Daane addresses this subject well. We will conclude this chapter with his observations:

'It is common in many evangelical circles to assert that the missionary, the evangelist and the occupant of the congregational pulpit must "preach for decision". Yet, strangely and significantly, this "preaching for decision" does not actually happen until *after* the sermon is finished in an "altar call". Many who proclaim the gospel make the appeal to their hearers to make a decision for Christ not in and through and by means of the preaching of the Word, but in the period that follows the sermon, using such means as lowering the house lights, asking that all heads be bowed and all eyes closed — not, as one might expect, for prayer but for hearing persuasive words and emotional appeals — while a choir may softly sing "Just As I Am, Without One Plea" (though the speaker is doing the best job of pleading he can) or some comparable song.

If ministers would *preach* for decisions for Christ, things would be better than they are. But is the elaborate altar call not really a denial that "faith comes from what is heard, and what is heard comes by the preaching of Christ" (Rom. 10:17)? Surely people who are converted should stand up to be counted and publicly confess their faith in Christ. But the effort to effect conversions in an altar-call period after the preaching is finished would seem to be an unspoken, perhaps unconscious admission that one does not believe the preached Word has the power to convert and save. If faith, as Paul teaches, comes through the hearing of Christ preached, what more is needed? To think that more than preaching is required, that altar call must follow sermon to render the preached Word effective, betrays a lack of faith in the mysterious, creative, saving power of the Word of God, qualities which no other words possess, not even those well-intended human words heard in an altar call.

The church in our time needs nothing more than a renewal of faith in the power of the proclamation of the Word of God. A Word that works faith in sinners and saves them without their prior permission may offend sinners, and a Word that saves people through its human proclamation without additional words of persuasion and pleading may offend even the preacher of the evangel. But it is faith and only faith alone which acknowledges that character of the gospel which offends sinners; and faith and only faith which can overcome that sense of offence because it alone acknowledges that what a person is offended at is an echo of the grace of God, a form of saving judgement and a grace that alone can save.

What Christian would deny that he or she once resisted

the gospel and was offended by it and still has moments which are not wholly free of such reactions? But if that is how things are, is "decision" the most appropriate term for conversion? Is the conversion experience not described more exactly by such terms as surrender to God and cessation of hostility and resistance to Christ — the attitude which confesses, "Nothing in my hand I bring" — not even my decision. Such a capitulation in faith more truly depicts the gospel's demand for obedience than does a presentation of the gospel which provides the sinner with options for decision.'[3]

Footnotes
1. D. Martyn Lloyd-Jones, *Preaching and Preachers,* Hodder and Stoughton, pp. 271–282.
2. John Stott, *I Believe in Preaching,* Hodder and Stoughton, p. 69ff.
3. James Daane, *Preaching with Confidence,* Eeerdmans, pp. 42–43.

10.
Four great preachers who did not use the invitation system

Why should we be concerned with four famous preachers who did not employ the public invitation system? After all, many well-known preachers use the method today. The question is not one of quoting big names for and against. Rather it is a matter of exploring the mentality of those who have not used the method in order to establish what makes the difference. It will help to discuss the subject in general before considering the outlook of William Perkins (1558–1602), Jonathan Edwards (1704–1758), C. H. Spurgeon (1835–1892) and Martyn Lloyd-Jones (1900-1981). Obviously the first two lived in times when the public appeal as a system of invitation did not exist, yet we can learn much from them with regard to our subject.

It should be noted that the use of the 'appeal' is not decided by the Calvinist-Arminian divide. Many Arminian preachers do not use the method because they are aware of the danger of encouraging false professions. It is true that Calvinists as a rule do not use it but some can be found who have used the appeal with discretion. Rolfe Barnard (1904–1969) was one such.[1]

Rolfe Barnard was a powerful preacher whose ministry was well known in America from about 1945–1965. Barnard placed a great emphasis on repentance. When he called for a visible response he was not impressed unless there was substantial evidence of repentance. Like John the Baptist he was only concerned with those who really meant to quit the world and follow Christ. Those who know America well will readily concede that culture plays a major role in the altar call. To describe the cultural aspect

is not easy. The people are tremendously outgoing. Unlike the British, who are mostly reserved by temperament, the extrovert factor is much higher among our American cousins, perhaps especially so in the Southern states. The ability to be uninhibited before other people in expressing feelings or ideas is a feature of culture. My view is that when Rolfe Barnard did make an 'appeal' this was largely a cultural thing, that is, the practice was expected. Some preachers have employed the altar call because that is what they have always known. They have inherited the concept and now move in that groove. T. T. Shields of Jarvis Street, probably the most famous preacher Canada has had, used this method. He was a fundamentalist. I have taken it for granted that my readers are familiar with the Calvinist/ Arminian issues, but they may not be sure about fundamentalism, especially since the term is often used in a derisive way to describe those who believe the Bible totally. A series of twelve booklets were published between 1910 and 1912 under the general heading *The Fundamentals: A Testimony to the Truth*. Nine fundamentals emerged in May 1919 when the World's Christian Fundamentals Association was formed with Dr W. B. Riley as its president. Members were required to be loyal to the following nine points:
1. The inspiration and inerrancy of Scripture;
2. the Trinity;
3. the deity and virgin birth of Christ;
4. the creation and fall of man;
5. Christ's substitionary atonement;
6. the bodily resurrection and ascension of Christ;
7. the regeneration of believers;
8. the imminent and personal return of Christ;
9. the resurrection, eternal blessedness for the redeemed and eternal woe for the unregenerate.

These points are indeed basic and T. T. Shields was faithful in preaching and defending these fundamentals. During the last two or three decades there has been an awakening in the Reformed faith, the doctrinal tenets of which are expressed in the Westminster Confession of Faith (Presbyterian) and the 1689 Confession of Faith (Baptist). Compared with a few lines of doctrine these statements spell out the great truths of the gospel in detail. Those who

cherish these Reformed confessions are aware of the fact
that they express the way of salvation in a structured form
which is beautiful in its harmony and closeness to Scripture.
It is not surprising that ministers who love the Reformed
faith are more sensitive than fundamentalists about the
issues surrounding the appeal. I hasten to add that in an
era of great confusion and apostasy from the gospel we are
thankful for all those who are loyal to the fundamentals.
We turn now to one of the fathers of the Reformed faith,
namely William Perkins.

I   William Perkins (1558-1602)

The need to discern the diversity of a congregation

William Perkins stands at the head of three generations of
Puritan divines — four, if we were to include the sons of
some Puritans, like Philip Henry, ejected with 2,000 others
in 1662. His son, Matthew Henry, became a famous com-
mentator on the whole Bible.

While there were many differences of viewpoint among
the Puritans on some issues of lesser importance, they were
united on the subject of salvation. The movement began
with those who taught patiently and long, men like Arthur
Hildesham, John Dod and Laurence Chaderton. The last-
named was the formative influence upon the life and thinking of William Perkins. Chaderton outlived Perkins by
thirty-eight years, dying in 1640 at the ripe old age of 103.
Chaderton was the first Master of Emmanuel College, which
became a citadel for English Puritanism.

Perkins was a graduate of Christ's College, Cambridge.
Before his conversion he was reckless and notorious for
his profanity and drunkenness. He was awakened spiritually
when he overhead a woman threaten her fretful child that
she would hand him over to 'Drunken Perkins'. After his

conversion, Perkins made rapid progress and became a famous preacher at the Church of the Greater St Andrews. People flocked to hear him preach. The students benefited greatly from his ministry. William Ames and John Robinson were among those moulded by him. Although he died aged only forty-four, his works were read more than any other theologian of his generation. They were also translated into many other languages. An interesting personal detail about Perkins is that he wrote everything with his left hand, because he had a disability in his natural writing hand.

Among his many writings, *The Art of Prophesying* was the first great and penetrating work on preaching since the Reformation. It was a masterly and profound treatise and could stand alongside any book on preaching written since that time. In many ways it is superior even to the best books on the subject of preaching today. R. T. Kendall says of this epoch-making discourse, 'It reveals the heart-beat of the man who shaped if not changed the style of preaching in England possibly more than any other.'[2]

In the *Art of Prophesying* Perkins described seven categories of hearers. Space will not allow us to do justice to the detail and care with which he thought his way through these groups of people who hear gospel preaching regularly. The categories are:

1. The unbelievers, who are both ignorant and unteachable.
2. Those who are teachable but yet ignorant.
3. Those who have knowledge but are not yet humbled.
4. Those who are humbled.
5. Those who do believe.
6. Those who are fallen.
7. Those who are 'mingled', by which Perkins means 'mixed'.

This principle of analysing the different spiritual conditions represented in a congregation is important. There are those who although they listen regularly are far from being teachable at the spiritual level of learning at the feet of Christ. All who are not humbled and needy have before anything else to be brought to conviction of their need and a sense of lostness. That kind of preaching which ignores the reality of sin is useless. It is essential that souls be awakened and be brought to an awesome encounter with God. First the wrath of God is revealed from heaven and then the righteousness of Christ.

When we consider the invitation system we see that it calls people to a profession of faith irrespective of whether the hearers have been truly brought face to face with God. Suddenly they are challenged to go through a process which leads to a false assurance and subsequent delusion. Of course, the hearer may be discerning enough to know that the process through which he passes is mechanical or he may have the advantage of Christian friends who can counsel him correctly and realistically.

Perkins also spoke of those who were humbled and ready to seek God. We take up that condition and make our observation that even when we are counselling seekers we can only employ the same terms used by our Lord, that is, we counsel seekers to press forward and call on the name of the Lord. We can never really be confident about people being born again until we see the fruit of the Spirit in them. If they rejoice in peace and assurance we can surely rejoice in that and have the highest of hopes, but only the Lord knows with absolute finality those who are his.

Taking up Perkins' example of analysing the congregation, we should be thankful that he reminds us of the importance of this. How many preachers today make the effort to think carefully about the different categories and needs of their hearers? Of course, if as preachers and pastors we pray for our people daily and concern ourselves intimately with their needs and the spiritual requirements of the relatives and friends they bring with them, we will be sensitive about all aspects of our presentation. We will study how we may best challenge all our hearers, from those who are ignorant to those who are spiritually mature.

A foremost factor in any congregation are the children and young people. Their response to an 'appeal' is much more ready than that of the more mature. Some ministers can point to young people who have gone forward in response to appeals on several occasions and most pastors are aware of individuals in their congregations who would respond easily to an appeal. By temperament there are always some who do not think about the details or implications. If they feel a moral pull they will readily respond to it, but that is not the same as conversion.

Among the different kinds of people are those who are naturally emotional and outgoing by temperament. Their demeanour has to be considered with regard to any kind of appeal that is made to them. In contrast to the outgoing there are those who are stubborn by nature and introverted. They make up their minds that they are not going to respond to any kind of appeal to stand or come to the front. Inwardly this may lead to a feeling of guilt. But guilt does not necessarily lie in failure to respond to an appeal. Guilt lies in sins committed in unbelief and in refusal to repent and obey the gospel.

To sum up, William Perkins provides a forceful reminder of the diversity of temperaments and spiritual conditions represented in any congregation. He reminds us too of the Puritan age, which was characterized by powerful preachers whose understanding of the Scriptures did not dispose them to invent anything resembling a public invitation to come forward.

Charles Bridges in *The Christian Ministry*[3] teaches the basic importance of a minister taking note of the various classes of people among whom he proclaims the gospel. The categories described by Bridges are

1. The infidel.
2. The ignorant and careless.
3. The self-righteous.
4. The false professor.
5. Those whose convictions are only natural.
6. Those who show spiritual convictions.
7. The young believers.
8. Backsliders.
9. The unestablished Christians.
10. Consistent Christians.

Whatever we say or do in our ministries must be suitable for all these classes of people. That is what makes the ministry an exacting work. Who is sufficient for these things? If we indulge in an 'appeal' we have to think of the short and long term effects of that upon all categories of our hearers. If we are sensitive to the different people in our congregations and the wide diversity of spiritual conditions and needs they represent, we will preach to meet those needs and at the same time promote in our congregations the principle of mature personal counselling, one to one, and not resort to the invitation system which by its haphazard nature cuts across that principle.

II   Jonathan Edwards (1703-1758)

Preparation for regeneration observed

Regarded as America's greatest theologian, Jonathan Edwards early showed his intellectual genius when he began his studies at Yale at the age of twelve. At the age of seventeen he gave his valedictory address in Latin. He pastored in New York for eight months and then in 1723 he returned to Yale as a tutor and worked there for three years. He was then called to Northampton where he was pastor for twenty-three years.

Edwards was a prodigious student. He rose early each day. By his own admission he did not devote much time to visitation, but rather spent most of his hours with his books. He would often miss his evening meal in preference for study. He kept physically fit. He watched his weight. He chopped wood in winter and went horse-riding in summer. Conflict arose between Edwards and his congregation when he attempted to bring reformation by restricting the communion table to believers only. This led to his being dismissed. This is astonishing when we recall that Edwards was greatly used in revival at Northampton and indeed was the principal instrument used by God in the Great Awakening in the New England States. Pre-eminently Edwards was the theologian of revival. His written works include *The Religious Affections*, a study of religious experience. This work is regarded by many as the finest ever produced on the subject. Edwards's writings, currently available in two large volumes from the Banner of Truth, have never been more relevant than they are today. Almost all the biblical emphases asserted by Edwards are neglected in our day. The observations of the Holy Spirit's work in revival gave him a vantage-point which he was uniquely able to employ in his writing on the anatomy of the soul and the way in which it is brought into a state of grace.

From Northampton Edwards moved to Stockbridge, where he worked as pastor of a small church and as a missionary among the Indians. His life was tragically and unexpectedly cut off when he reacted adversely to an innoculation for smallpox. With the medical expertise of our generation it would have been straightforward to rescue him, a fact which makes the recollection of his untimely death seem even more tragic. During the seven years at Stockbridge he was wonderfully productive and wrote incessantly. Yale University Press are at present publishing his complete works which go much further than the two large volumes already referred to, which are in double columns and small print. Yale plan to extend Edwards's works to fifty-four volumes, to be completed by the beginning of the next century.

We are going to take up just one aspect of Edwards's theology which touches our subject in a very practical way.

Edwards was in the fullest sense a preparationist. That term means that God prepares people for the new birth. This principle lies at the foundation of all that he wrote in *The Religious Affections*. The subject of preparationism is widely misunderstood. For this reason it is explained in detail in chapter 5. One of its main implications is that there is a great deal of religious feeling and experience which falls short of the new birth.

Edwards taught that great affections, effects on the body, fluency and fervour of speech or of expression, zeal and confidence, together with moving testimonies — all these can all fall short of the new birth.

It was his observation of the spiritual awakening that enabled him to trace out the Holy Spirit's consecutive or chronological work in a soul. Remembering that an unconverted person can advance in understanding, in transformation of life and in spiritual conviction, we must ask where is the line of new birth? A tension is always present because while we recognize the place of preparation, it is wrong to ignore the importance of urgency. It is always of the utmost urgency that a person outside of Christ repents and believes. Also we must always hold firmly to the truth that it is God who prepares people for the new birth. To the preacher belongs the sphere of teaching, preaching, exhortation and counselling. The Holy Spirit alone makes the work fruitful in the souls of the hearers.

Edwards observed a pattern which was typical and this he sought to describe. In observing a pattern in the Holy Spirit's work Edwards was insistent that the Holy Spirit did not bind himself to any one procedure. In one instant he can work in one person what he generally takes time to work in others. While there are consecutive steps to be observed in most cases of conversion, the Holy Spirit would in exceptional cases leap over all those steps. The very essence of preparation is that God is sovereign in his working in souls. In no way is he subject to our control or methods, to our mechanics, our timing or our methodology.

What, then, was the general pattern of the Holy Spirit's work observed by Edwards? The first step in the conversion process was an awakening to danger, a sense of horror at being eternally lost. The natural state of a soul in sin is one of extreme wretchedness and misery. The second step was a response by the awakened soul to this appalling state. There was a measure of reformation in the person awakened, seeking to avoid sins which would exacerbate that condition of guilt and lostness. Also there was a looking for a solution and a willingness to use the means of grace.

The next move, the third, was a conviction of absolute dependence on God's sovereign power and grace. The source of help became clear. One would think that immediate refuge in God would be resorted to at this stage, but it was not always so. Recourse by the awakened was to their own strength and ability to find God. In this exercise they did not find the peace they were seeking. In the fruitlessness of their own endeavours a new conviction overcame them, namely, that God was just in their condemnation. He did not have to save them. He was not obliged to do so. Their own performances were futile. This was the fourth stage and it prepared the way for the dawning for the first time of the glory of God. The awakened soul began 'to see feelingly' or to be moved by the beauty of God. To Edwards this fifth stage was absolutely crucial. To him gracious religious affections were bedded in a person having a truly inward love for the moral excellence and glorious attributes of God. It is not enough for sinners to see God as the source and centre of their own need, as if his existence were merely to meet their desires and satisfy their convenience. Reality is to see and appreciate the Godhood of God.

All these five steps Edwards esteemed as 'preparatory to grace'. Again it is imperative to stress that these five steps were not a human work pushed forward and organized by the sinner and aided by his pastor as counsellor. All preparatory work is by the Spirit.

The next stage, the sixth, 'is an earnest longing of the soul after God and Christ'. This desire is the very opposite of that of the natural man, who is at enmity to God. It is one thing to recognize God's glory; it is another to desire him. The seventh stage was one in which the awakened soul reposed in Christ and became aware of being delighted in Christ.

The eighth step was assurance. Edwards regarded assurance as vital. A lack of assurance could hinder spiritual growth. Assurance which did not result in obedience and Christian practice was not genuine.[4]

We have observed the progress of a soul towards salvation and, whatever differences we may have about the details, the important question must be asked: where does the modern invitation system fit into Edwards's understanding and observations? The method used today is one which dispenses with this idea of preparation by God. Results can be had on the spot. The prevalent idea is that of immediate results by inducing a decision for God as if it were just a matter of my deciding right now that I have God.

Again, lest anyone misunderstand, I say that we must always set Christ before men and urge that they come to him and close with him. Yet we must remember that God is not an automatic dispensing machine. There is the seeker on the one hand and a sovereign God on the other.

It would be a mistake to think of the sovereignty in such a way that we conclude that we have no part to play.

God will do it all! God will certainly begin and complete his work in the souls of men, but he uses means. Especially does he use preachers. Edwards himself is an excellent example of this. Edwards was passionate. He pleaded with men. He did not hesitate to threaten. For him eternity was at stake. I have mentioned that he was an incessant writer. He was also an accurate writer, which is why there is so much of value to print. A contemporary described Edwards's eloquence like this: 'His eloquence was the power of presenting an important truth before an audience with overwhelming weight of argument, and with such intenseness of feeling that the whole soul of the speaker was thrown into every part of the conception and delivery, so that the solemn attention of the whole audience was rivetted from the beginning to the close so that the impressions could not be effaced.'[5] Edwards was hostile to dull, lethargic preaching.

Enough has been presented to show that any method or formula or institutionalized means of getting people to make decisions would find no quarter with Jonathan Edwards.

III   Charles Haddon Spurgeon (1834-1892)

The power of preaching is adequate

What Charles Haddon Spurgeon said of John Wycliffe is true of himself: 'God fits the man for the place and the place for the man; there is an hour for the voice and a voice for the hour.' The truth of this statement concerning the voice, the hour and the place was wonderfully exemplified in the case of Spurgeon as a great preacher and writer. He was the instrument of countless conversions. It is remarkable that almost a century after his passing, Spurgeon still has a great influence among Baptists. Born in 1834 at Kelvedon, Essex, Spurgeon was converted in a little

Methodist chapel on a cold wintry day, 6 January 1850. He was baptized in the beautiful river Lark which forms the border between Cambridgeshire and Suffolk. That was just a few weeks before his sixteenth birthday. Soon after, in a jacket and turned-down collar, he preached his first sermon in a cottage at Teversham before a group of farm labourers and villagers. No sooner had he finished than an old lady exclaimed, 'Bless your dear heart, how old are you?' Spurgeon's solemn answer was that the service must conclude before enquiries of that nature could take place. The old lady was determined and repeated the question the moment after the benediction. 'How old are you?' she insisted. 'I am under sixty!' replied the boy preacher. 'Yes, and under sixteen too!' was the old lady's rejoinder.

The fact is that his eloquence and unction had immediately been recognized. This was to be the pattern thereafter. In April 1854 Spurgeon was called to be pastor of Waterbeach Baptist Chapel, near Cambridge. Five and a half years later he was called to the New Park Street Chapel, Southwark, London. It was a church with a great history, but was run down and in decline. If ever a preacher took a city by storm Spurgeon did. Never was there a young expositor of such quality as he. His youth was part of the attraction. However, his doctrine aroused bitter opposition. Caricature and calumny by the press combined in an effort to destroy his effectiveness, but to no avail for the crowds increased. Large halls were hired, including the Surrey Gardens Music Hall, which was filled with 10,000 hearers. Eventually the Metropolitan Tabernacle was built, seating 6,000, and to the end of his life Spurgeon used to fill that Victorian structure with its two decks of circular galleries built round a large open pulpit. Westminster Chapel, Buckingham Gate, is a smaller version of the same style and interior design.

When I first entered the ministry we had an aged trustee, Mr C. W. J. Leake, who lived to an advanced age. He described to me his impression of Spurgeon's preaching. He said his rich resonant voice was like the pealing of a golden bell which instantly gripped people when they heard it. His voice was the voice for that hour. What a pity they did not have tape-recording in those days, because we could then hear that prince of preachers! While we have not inherited a cassette service, we do possess from Spurgeon the most comprehensive set of sermons in print ever bequeathed to the church by a preacher. By 1899 over one hundred million of his sermons had been published in twenty-three languages. There are now sixty volumes of his sermons in print. For twenty-seven years Spurgeon edited *The Sword and the Trowel,* which provides a further source of material. One hundred and twenty-five other books and booklets bear his name. One hundred and twenty thousand copies of his large five-volume commentary on the Psalms *The Treasury of David* sold before his death.

From these resources we are well able to determine Spurgeon's methods and views. We can easily ascertain how he invited lost sinners to Christ. From the great corpus of recorded sermons we can determine whether he ever used the 'appeal' or invited his hearers to an enquiry room.

It will help us at this point to recall that there were three great controversies in Spurgeon's life. The first resulted from Spurgeon's preaching, in which he vigorously exposed the flabby and diluted evangelism of his day. The second came about as a result of a sermon preached on 5 June 1864, which attacked baptismal regeneration. This resulted in a furore and much debate. The third concerned the rising tide of modernism or liberalism, which involved Spurgeon in an exhausting battle from 1887 until his death in 1892. This last struggle is known as 'The Downgrade Controversy'.

The first of these debates relates to our subject. It involves the whole question of Calvinism and Arminianism. It is not possible to understand these issues properly unless we come to terms with the fact that Spurgeon was a Puritan in his thinking and practice. He loved the whole Puritan period of 1558 to 1662 and beyond. He admired the Puritan writers, having discovered them in his grandfather's library as a child, and read them deeply and constantly. His book *Commenting and Commentaries,* in which he commends countless Puritan authors, illustrates his massive and retentive knowledge of Puritan books. He discovered, as have many in our day, that the Puritans as a class of expositors and pastors were in a category of their own. For a combination of doctrine, experiential religion and practical holy living, they are outstanding. Jonathan Edwards, whom we have thought about, and Dr Martyn Lloyd-Jones, to whom we will turn separately, both made Puritan literature their priority. They mingled constantly with mighty theological intellects and themselves grew in stature thereby.

We must now grapple with our principal subject — why Spurgeon did not use the 'appeal'. R. T. Kendall quotes Dr Eric Hayden, a former minister of the Metropolitan Tabernacle, as maintaining that the architectural layout in the Tabernacle was unsuitable for people to walk to the front and that that is why Spurgeon did not do it.[6] My response to that is that the reason for Spurgeon not using the invitation system lay in his theology and had nothing whatever to do with architecture.

R. T. Kendall also points out that he invited D. L. Moody to preach at the Tabernacle and claims this shows that he was not opposed to the 'appeal' procedures. However, we all know that you do not have to agree with everything a preacher does or says before you invite him to your pulpit. The relationship of Spurgeon with Moody is a large subject which is analysed in detail by Iain Murray in his book *The Forgotten Spurgeon.*[7] The well-known preacher of Scotland, John Kenneddy of Dingwall, did analyse Moody's theology and methods thoroughly and warned against wrong methods in evangelism. John Kenneddy was censored fiercely by many because he exposed the weaknesses of Moody's methods, whereupon Kenneddy was defended by Spurgeon. The dilemma which faced Spurgeon is one which faces all pastors who do not believe in the methods used by some evangelists. The problem is one of sorting out a mixed blessing and weighing up the credit side against the debit side. Added to this is the tremendous problem of appearing to oppose soul-winning or be in opposition to evangelism when nothing is further from the truth.

R. T. Kendall also points to the fact that some (how many has not been documented) of Spurgeon's evangelists used the invitation system, because there are reports in the *Sword and Trowel* to that effect. In response to this I ask whether it is reasonable to expect that workers who may have been trained in Spurgeon's College, or who were supported by Tabernacle funds would necessarily have precisely the same judgement or mentality as their mentor? You cannot stop men using methods different from your own, especially if they have not grasped for themselves the issues that lie at the root of the practices in question.

The fact that Spurgeon did not use the invitation system is clearly established by an examination of his sermons. We have 3,000 and in each case we can see how the preacher concluded. There is no evidence of an appeal for people to come to the front or any semblance of an invitation system.

That the membership of the Tabernacle was not accustomed to the invitation system is mentioned by Alan Streett in his book.[8] Dr A. C. Dixon (1854–1925), an American pastor-evangelist from North Carolina, was called to what we now call Spurgeon's Tabernacle in 1911. Streett maintains that Dixon received much criticism when he began calling people 'to come forward and accept Christ'. Says Streett, 'The British were not accustomed to such a bold and direct invitation.' The story of the decline at Spurgeon's Tabernacle is brilliantly narrated by Iain Murray in *The Forgotten Spurgeon*[9], a book which should be a text-book and made required reading for every Baptist student in every Baptist college throughout the world. The aftermath at the Metropolitan Tabernacle is similar in many ways to the changes that have recently taken place at Westminster Chapel, London. The parallels are striking.[10]

The tide was increasingly against Puritan theology in the latter half of Spurgeon's life. It is doubtful whether it was ever strong during that period. Strangely Spurgeon, while drinking at the well of Puritanism himself, was not the best promoter of Puritan theology. Certainly he constantly recommended Puritan literature, but his own expository method did not follow the Puritan method of preaching through the books of the Bible systematically. There were specific reasons which disposed Spurgeon to his method. This is a fascinating subject and I must not digress now to analyse it. How many of his hearers really understood the doctrines of grace and their implications is a question difficult to answer. That a great falling away from Puritanism took place from the time of Spurgeon's death until the 1960s is indisputable.

Did Spurgeon say anything explicit on the 'appeal' and

enquiry room? Yes, he did. As that system became more popular he spoke clearly against it. In an address with the title 'The Minister in these times' he warned: 'Let me say, very softly and whisperingly, that there are little things among ourselves which must be carefully looked after, or we shall have a leaven of Ritualism and priesthood working in our measures of meal. In our revival services, it might be as well to vary our procedure. Sometimes shut up that enquiry room. I have my fears about that institution if it be used in permanence, and as an inevitable part of the services. It may be a very wise thing to invite persons who are under concern of soul to come apart from the rest of the congregation, and have conversation with godly people; but if you should ever see a notion is fashioning itself that there is something to be got in the private room which is not to be had at once in the assembly, or that God is more at that penitent form than elsewhere, aim a blow at that notion at once. We must not come back by a rapid march to the old ways of altars and confessionals, and have a Romish trumpery restored in a coarser form. If we make men think that conversation with ourselves or with our helpers is essential to their faith in Christ, we are taking the direct line for priestcraft. In the Gospel, the sinner and the Saviour are to come together, with none between. Speak upon this point very clearly. "You, sinner, sitting where you are, believing on the Lord Jesus Christ, shall have eternal life. Do not stop till you pass into an enquiry room. Do not think it essential to confer with me. Do not suppose that I have the keys of the Kingdom of Heaven, or that these godly men and women associated with me can tell you any other Gospel than this. He that believeth on the Son hath everlasting life." '[11]

Also in his preaching he said concerning convicted sinners: 'Go home alone, trusting in Jesus. [Spurgeon now quotes the sinner.] "I would like to go into the enquiry room." I dare say you would, but we are not willing to pander to popular superstition. We fear that in those rooms men are warmed into fictitious confidence. Very few of the supposed converts of enquiry rooms turn out well. Go to your God at once, even where you are now. Cast yourself on Christ, now, at once, ere you stir an inch!'

A recurring warning in his later sermons was 'God has not appointed salvation by enquiry rooms . . . For the most part, a wounded conscience, like a wounded stag, delights to be alone that it may bleed in secret.'

Then in *The Soul Winner*[12] Spurgeon declares: 'All hurry to get members into the church is most mischievous, both to the church and to the supposed converts . . . Some of the most glaring sinners known to me were once members of a church, and were, as I believe, led to make a profession by undue pressure, well-meant but ill-judged . . . What mean these despatches from the battlefield, "Last night fourteen souls were under conviction, fifteen were justified, and eight received full sanctification"? I am weary of this public bragging, this counting of unhatched chickens, this exhibition of doubtful spoils. Lay aside such numberings of the people, such idle pretence of certifying in half a minute that which will need the testing of a lifetime. Hope for the best, but in your highest excitements be reasonable. Enquiry rooms are all very well, but if they lead to idle boastings they will grieve the Holy Spirit and work abounding evil . . . Do not aim at sensation and "effect". Flowing tears and streaming eyes, sobs and outcries, and crowded after-meetings and all kinds of confusions may occur, and may be borne with as concomitants of genuine feeling, but pray do not plan their production . . . No one is more sorry than I that such a caution as this should be needful, but in the presence of certain wild revivalists, I cannot say less and might say a great deal more.' This same quotation is found in the 1879 volume of sermons under the title, 'What it is to win a soul'.

We still have not specified precisely why Spurgeon did not employ the invitation system. The direct answer to that is that he believed that the Holy Spirit uses preaching to raise the dead. That means is adequate. We should not seek to do the Holy Spirit's work for him. Souls are born again in their seats under the proclamation of the gospel.

Dr Lloyd-Jones, whose life and ministry we are going to look at next, always laid great stress on the centrality of preaching. He was hostile towards anything which threatened the primacy of preaching. Likewise Spurgeon was against anything which usurped the role of preaching.

Moody, by way of contrast, championed the enquiry room
and, according to R. T. Kendall said, 'In my own experience
I find that where one person has been converted under the
sermon, a hundred have been converted in the enquiry
room.'[13] That is very telling because it forms its own commentary on the mechanism of decision-making. It illustrates
the widespread assumption that if people are taken through
four easy steps then that constitutes conversion.

In 1857 Spurgeon reported that it was his happiness to
see personally not less than 1,000 who had been converted
under his ministry.[14] We should note that in Spurgeon's
ministry it was under the preaching that these conversions
took place. The converts emerged in the glory of God's
strength to testify of what the Lord had done for them.

We should observe too that 1857 was a time of spiritual
revival. We are compelled to take note of God's sovereignty.
There are times of sowing and times of reaping. Often when
the going is exacting and tiring, instead of persevering in
the hard work of constant evangelistic outreach, the evangelical churches organize their own so-called revivals. These
are of human manufacture. The church in our day has lost
power, abandoning the acknowledgement of the sovereignty
of God. The old way was earnestly to seek the. Lord for the
outpouring of his Spirit. Revivals in those times were
frequent but awesome encounters with the living God.

There is surely a direct connection between doctrine
and experience and vice-versa. Doctrine which is balanced
and thorough will maintain biblical standards for conversion
and the church will be preserved from those coming into
her ranks who are merely converts of human enterprise.
Experience of revival brings men and women to realize the
holiness of God. They are endued with discernment which
recognizes the true from the false.

In his early days C. H. Spurgeon particularly enjoyed
times of refreshing from the presence of the Lord. Those
were times of reaping. In his later years he saw much drift-
ing away from the old standards. He found he had to defend
the authority of Scripture itself. Nevertheless he was bold
to affirm his faith in the future, believing that God's truth
would be restored in God's time. He declared, 'The doctrine
which is now rejected as the effete theory of Puritans and

Calvinists will yet conquer human thought and reign supreme. As surely as the sun which sets tonight shall rise tomorrow at the predestined hour, so shall the truth of God shine forth over the whole earth.'[15]

We are grateful for Spurgeon. May his optimistic prediction be fulfilled in this generation.

IV   D. Martyn Lloyd-Jones (1900-1981)

Preaching to convert the whole person and not just his will

Born in 1900, Dr Martyn Lloyd-Jones enjoyed a long and rich ministry. In spite of the fact that his books have spread widely, there are many, especially overseas, who know little of the life of this outstanding preacher and leader. Even in his native Wales, where he preached to large congregations, I have come across those who have never heard of him. The famous and extensive St Deiniol's Library, established and endowed by the Prime Minister W. E. Gladstone (1809– 1898), did not have a single entry for D. Martyn Lloyd-Jones — a deficiency which has now been rectified!

Martyn Lloyd-Jones came from rural Wales as a young man to embark on a medical career in London. At the age of twenty-three he was chief clinical assistant to Sir Thomas Horder, the King's Physician. At twenty-seven he shocked many by giving up lucrative prospects as a physician and accepting a call to become the minister of a struggling Calvinistic Methodist Chapel at Aberavon, South Wales.

Early in his Christian experience 'the doctor' was influenced by the Puritans, especially John Owen. He describes too how he made the wonderful discovery of the two large volumes of the *Works of Jonathan Edwards*, which he commended to preachers as the best material that they could possibly possess.

When he took up the pastorate at Sandfields, Aberavon,

he referred to our Puritan forbears and advocated a return
to their biblical attitudes. Writing in 1927, the former pastor,
E. T. Rees, declared that 'the penitent form' and 'the pledge'
were gone! No one was summoned to 'come forward'. The
same writer also testified, 'Our Sunday services are warm,
hearty and helpful, and many find their way to the
Master.'[16]

By 1933 newspapers reported that Lloyd-Jones was drawing thousands from all parts of Wales to hear his message.
It is significant to note that there is not one preacher in
the United Kingdom today (1985), who has the gifts to do
that on his own, that is without the apparatus of an evangelistic organization.

In 1935 the doctor began a lifelong involvement with the
Inter-Varsity Fellowship. He became president of the I.V.F.
in 1939. His influence on the movement was crucial. He
was the principal instrument in bringing that body from a
non-intellectual approach to one which was solidly doctrinal.
It was imperative that the I.V.F. should overcome the
dominance of the modernist Student Christian Movement.

In 1939 Dr Martyn Lloyd-Jones accepted a call to Westminster Chapel, London, where he laboured alongside
G. Campbell Morgan until the latter's retirement in 1943.
Altogether the doctor was to minister at Westminster Chapel
for twenty-nine years. His effectiveness in the heart of the
capital city during that time was tremendous. Besides
influencing students from all over the world, he encouraged
a fraternal of ministers which grew to a regular monthly
attendance of about 180 to 200. This was called the Westminster Fraternal. He was also instrumental in sponsoring
the annual Puritan Study Conference at Westminster Chapel.
This began with a little group in the early 1950s but has
grown to about 200 and continues to be well supported.
It is now called the Westminster Conference. It was the
custom for the doctor to give the concluding address. Some
of his best expositions were given at those occasions. The
papers were printed annually.

While he came from Welsh Calvinistic stock, the doctor
was a Puritan to the marrow. This is seen in the all-round
balanced pastoral approach and is exemplified best in his
pastoral books such as *Spiritual Depression*. The two volumes

on *The Sermon on the Mount* represent his best work. Most of all it was his skill and unction in systematic, expository preaching that revived that art among countless ministers. Through ill-health he was obliged to retire in 1968 from the exacting toils of the regular preaching ministry at Westminster. After his retirement he recovered from a serious operation and in that same year lectured on the subject of preaching at Westminster Seminary in Philadelphia, Pennsylvania.

These lectures were published as a book, with the title *Preaching and Preachers*, which contains a chapter on 'Calling for Decisions'. In this exposition the doctor elaborates ten reasons why he did not believe in that system. As is typical of the preacher, some of the points tend to blend into each other:

1. Man consists of mind, affections and will. It is wrong to bypass the mind and affections in order merely to move the will.

2. Too much pressure on the will is dangerous because the response will then be one governed by influences other than the truth, i.e. the personality of the preacher or stirring music.

3. The preaching of the Word and the call for decision should not be separated. It is a Reformed principle that no sacrament be developed which is separate from preaching. (I explain this in my section on a new evangelical sacrament. The doctor adds later, on p. 282, that there should be application all the way through a sermon. The appeal should be implicit throughout.)

4. The idea that sinners can decide 'just like that!' is basically unbiblical.

5. The idea that the evangelist is in a position to manipulate the Holy Spirit is wrong.

6. The method tends to produce a superficial conviction of sin, if any at all.

7. The idea that somehow the act of going forward saves is an erroneous one.

8. The invitation system is by its very nature a system of distrust, as though the Holy Spirit needed this supplement, this aid and help. Later, on page 282, he concludes

the whole by saying, 'Do not force these things. This
is the work of the Holy Spirit of God. His work is a
thorough work, it is a lasting work; and so we must
not yield to this over-anxiety about results.'

9.   It undermines the doctrine of regeneration. No one
can do the work of the Holy Spirit for him. (Who
can say this is the moment if the Spirit does not design
that to be the moment?)

10. This is basically an opening up of point 4 and an exposition of it.

He concludes with many observations, one paragraph
of which deserves our careful attention. It reads: 'Moreover, I find in ministers' meetings, and in private conversation with many ministers, that in general, ministers find
their problems have increased rather than decreased in
recent years. I have already mentioned the case of men
who cannot even get a call from certain churches because
of this. I have spoken of others who are criticized by their
members because they do not make this 'call' at every
service. The practice seems to have introduced a new kind
of mentality, a carnality expressing itself as an unhealthy
interest in numbers. It has led also to a desire for excitement, and to an impatience almost with the message because
they are waiting for the "call" at the end and seeing of the
results. All this is surely very serious.'[17]

Of all points the doctor himself stresses the primacy of
the new birth. The doctrine of the sovereignty of the Holy
Spirit in regeneration enters into all ten points either
directly or indirectly and is expressly asserted in point nine.
While that is surely correct, our attention is certainly gripped
by the power of his first point. Who can escape the reality
and urgency of it? It is utterly self-defeating to press a man
in his volition or will to make a decision and then tell him
he is converted if his mind is not regenerated. When his
present feelings and emotions subside he will return to
what he was before. How many countless times have evangelicals experienced disappointment in this system of pressing
people for decisions? Yet, amazingly, they will still go on
using the system.

Not only is there a man's mind; there is his 'heart'. This
is the term used frequently in Scripture to denote the seat

of a person's affections. What a person loves determines what he will do. His primary need is to love God. For that he must be born again. To propel people along without dealing thoroughly with their hearts is self-defeating.

That is why Dr Lloyd-Jones, along with all those in the Puritan tradition, concentrated in preaching on persuading the mind and, through the mind, persuading the heart, looking to the Holy Spirit during all the exercises of preaching to quicken minds and hearts.

The reason why the Puritan preacher can have peace when he has completed his task is that he knows God will do his own work and that which he begins, he completes. In contrast to that, the invitation system relies too heavily on the method. Thus Streett in his book, in an effort to show how wrong Dr Lloyd-Jones was, is unscrupulous in deliberately cutting short a paragraph and omitting what follows.

But first we quote Streett: 'Dr D. Martyn Lloyd-Jones tells of an experience he had some years ago. One Sunday evening as he was delivering his sermon he noticed a man weeping in the audience. Although Lloyd-Jones sensed an urge to speak to the man about his soul at the close of the sermon, he held his peace. The following evening, the preacher happened to meet this same man along the roadway. Lloyd-Jones continues the story: 'He came across the road to me and said, "You know, doctor, if you had asked me to stay behind last night I would have done so." "Well," I said, "I am asking you now, come with me now." "Oh no," he replied, "but if you had asked me last night I would have done so." '[18]

Now note what follows in the original text, directly in mid-paragraph so Streett could not possibly have missed it: '". . . I would have done so!" "My dear friend," I said, "I am asking you now." "Oh no," he replied, "but if you had asked me last night I would have done so." "My dear friend," I said, "if what happened to you last night does not last for twenty-four hours I am not interested in it. If you are not as ready to come with me now as you were last night you have not got the right, the true thing. Whatever affected you last night was only temporary and passing, you still do not see your real need of Christ." '[19]

We are not to think that Dr Lloyd-Jones did not believe in counselling concerned souls. He always received people in his vestry after services. One Friday evening after an ordinary exposition with no pressure or special pleading at all, five people came in to see him, one after another. Each one was concerned about salvation. I remember the doctor saying that there was nothing special about that exposition.

To sum up Dr Lloyd-Jones' teaching on the subject, we see that he regarded the new birth as the crucial issue. That is evident as we study his expositions. However, the point that comes through with great impact is that we should not bypass the mind or the heart as we appeal to men. We can win them emotionally. We can persuade their wills temporarily. When the emotion is over and when the aura of the meeting is past they find that they are not at all convinced. Their hearts are not won. The exercise has been without profit and, as we shall see in the last chapter, can be fraught with all kinds of dangers. Substantial damage can be done. It is better therefore to cling to the means of grace that have been provided and add no invitation system of our own.

Footnotes
1. For biography see John F. Thornbury, *Reformation Today*, No. 45.
2. *Preaching and Revival*, The Westminster Conference Papers for 1984, p. 18.
3. Charles Bridges, *The Christian Ministry*, Banner of Truth, 1976, p. 344ff.
4. For a detailed study of this theme see Samuel T. Logan's treatise on Edwards given at the Westminster Conference, 1984, the title being 'Preaching and Revival'.
5. This quotation is from a cassette recording of John Piper's address on Edwards given at a college in Chicago.
6. *Stand up and be Counted*, p. 56.
7. Iain Murray, *The Forgotten Spurgeon*, Banner of Truth, p. 170ff.
8. *The Effective Invitation*, p. 102.
9. *The Forgotten Spurgeon*, p. 209ff.
10. *Stand up and be Counted*, p. 9ff. Dr Kendall describes how the change came as from April 1982.
11. C. H. Spurgeon, *An All Round Ministry*, Banner of Truth, p. 372.

12. *The Soul Winner.* Also see sermon in Metropolitan Pulpit, 1879, with title, 'What it is to win a soul'.
13. *Stand up and be Counted,* p. 55.
14. *The Forgotten Spurgeon,* p. 27.
15. Metropolitan Tabernacle Pulpit, vol. 23, p. 514, vol. 32, p. 91.
16. Iain Murray, *The First Forty Years,* Banner of Truth, p. 143.
17. Dr D. Martyn Lloyd-Jones, *Preaching and Preachers,* Hodder, p. 281.
18. *The Effective Invitation,* p. 175.
19. *Preaching and Preachers,* p. 276.

11.
Is the 'appeal' a harmful practice?

There are many ways in which we can admire the divine perfections of the life of Christ. He was God manifest in the flesh (1 Tim. 3:16). We see his deity shining in his miracles. We see it too in his sinless life. In him was no sin, neither did any deceit or untruth ever come from his lips. Likewise the methods he employed were pure. He could never be accused of duplicity. No person will ever be able to say that he has been deceived by Christ. No individual will ever be able to claim that he had been led by Christ to expect blessings on certain conditions which in the event never materialized.

When we come to examine the 'appeal' then the charge has to be made that as a system it does not measure up to the standards of honesty and truth that are found in the Bible. As a method it deceives and disillusions many. That is a strong charge to make. It requires substantiation. First we will look at the question of the harm done by the invitation system to individuals and then at the subject as it relates to the churches.

1. Does the 'appeal' harm individuals?

It will help us if we analyse the various reasons why people go forward, make a decision and are thereby assured that all is well, who are thereafter fatally disappointed.

Firstly, there are many who have a sense of remorse about sin. They appreciate that harm has been done to themselves and others. They grieve about the damage their sin has done.

159

Going forward at a meeting, in the minds of some, is like an act of penance which is regarded as a help to putting things right. However well-intentioned, such regret about sin falls short of repentance. 'Against you, you only have I sinned and done what is evil in your sight,' said David. Observe the Godward aspect of his confession. Sin is committed against heaven and against a holy God. A person can be sorry for the pain he has caused to himself, to his wife or to his family, but that is not repentance towards God. Those who are motivated by inward feelings of this kind are particularly prone to respond to an 'appeal'.

Secondly there are many who rightly and naturally fear death, the judgement, retribution and hell. It is natural to want to escape the horrors of a lost eternity. That is a good thing. We should have a realistic view of hell, but if this is something that springs only from a self-centred basis it is inadequate. Repentance is towards God. It is not mere self-pity. It is dangerous to think in terms of an easy way of deliverance from God's wrath. To escape the penalty of sin represents a great salvation. To be sure that we will escape hell is an immeasurable blessing. However, this escape should never be presented as something which can be gained easily without the cost of discipleship.

There is a parallel between the invitation system, with its quick and easy decision, which in most instances bypasses true repentance, and the complaint made by Jeremiah when he said of the false prophets of his day:

> 'They dress the wound of my people
>   as though it were not serious.
> 'Peace, peace,' they say,
>   when there is no peace'
>   (Jer. 6:14; 8:11).

The same bypassing of the necessity of repentance is seen in nominal religion, especially Roman Catholicism. Souls are taught to put their trust in the church as an institution and in the sacraments, especially baptism and the mass. They are never truly confronted with the necessity of repentance towards God, the new birth, justification by faith and the kind of holy life that is built on union with Christ.

There is a third category of people, a numerous constituency, who genuinely seek practical solutions to their personal or family problems. They observe that their Christian friends do seem to have joy, love and happiness. They admire them and often feel attracted to some of the beautiful aspects of Christianity. Many of these entertain a romantic idea of conversion and often possess an aesthetic admiration for that which is spiritually pure and good. They are particularly susceptible to the invitation system as they think that going forward and making a decision will in itself do something wonderful for them. Hopefully for them much that has been wrong will fall into place. This idea of an easy solution is characteristic of much present-day thinking, in which people look for simple and easy solutions to their problems, and when much of the advertising on the mass-media conveys the notion of simple solutions.

My observation is that many respond to the call to the front with this mentality, namely that problems will be solved by going forward. This does not begin to constitute true repentance towards God or saving faith in our Lord Jesus Christ. A system which is designed to get as many forward as possible and to produce as many professions as possible, by its very nature, bypasses these ingrained erroneous attitudes, which can only be eradicated by thorough pastoral work and a diligent preaching ministry.

For these reasons many who go through this process of decision-making go away thinking that the decision in itself will solve their problems, whereas it is the constant discipline of a teaching ministry, as is stressed in Matthew 28:18–20, that alone will meet these needs. When we follow the experiences of the vast majority we discover that they were led to believe that something really significant or wonderful would happen, but it did not. They remained unchanged and their problems were not alleviated in the least. A variety of reactions followed, from disillusionment to resentment, depending on the person involved. Some of the responses are described well by Robert L. Dabney (1820–1898), one of the foremost evangelical and Reformed theologians in the United States of America in the last century.

'Some [of those who have been counselled]', says Dabney, 'feel that a cruel trick has been played upon their inexperience by the ministers and friends of Christianity in thus thrusting them, in the hour of their confusion, into false positions, whose duties they do not and cannot perform, and into sacred professions which they have been compelled shamefully to repudiate. Their self-respect is therefore galled to the quick, and pride is indignant at the humiliating exposure. No wonder that they look on religion and its advocates henceforward with suspicion and anger. Often their feelings do not stop here. They are conscious that they were thoroughly in earnest in their religious anxieties and resolves at the time, and that they felt strange and profound exercises. Yet bitter and mortifying experience has taught them that their new birth and experimental religion at least was a delusion. How natural to conclude that those of all others are delusions also? They say, "The only difference between myself and these earnest Christians is, that they have not yet detected the cheat as I have. They are now not a whit more convinced of their sincerity and of the reality of their exercises than I once was of mine. Yet I know there was no change in my soul; I do not believe that there is in theirs."

Such is the fatal process of thought through which thousands have passed; until the country is sprinkled all over with infidels, who have been made such by their own experience of spurious religious excitements. They may keep their hostility to themselves in the main; because Christianity now "walks in her silver slippers", but they are not the less steeled against all saving impressions of the truth.'[1]

We should note that reactions are different. Some, as Dabney points out, become cynical and believe that the whole experience was a delusion. They come to regard the organizers as people themselves deceived.

As I said at the beginning of this chapter, we should never be guilty of propagating deception. It is not good enough for those who support the invitation system to say the whole exercise is worth it for the few for whom it does work. Nobody should go away confused or deceived because false hopes were held out. Yes, it is true that, because the heart of man is deceitful, some will abuse the gospel whatever way it is presented, but I maintain that we should never tolerate a system which by its very nature deceives multitudes.

I have not attempted to discuss other reasons why people respond to an 'appeal'. Some, particularly young people, say that they did it out of curiosity, or because they did not want to be left out, or even for a laugh, which is their way of expressing daring. They did it out of a sense of adventure. Those who do such things do not know what they are doing and as a result are unlikely to be scarred by the experience, although mature believers should be watchful to warn young people of the serious nature of these issues.

There is only one way to preach the gospel and that is to proclaim it with such clarity that the doors of the kingdom are shown to be open always, together with the instructions as to how a safe entrance is to be made. People should never be led into a trap by which they think that they have made an attempt which failed and that is the end of the matter. Not all, by any means, do think in that way. There are those who respond over and over again to the 'appeal'. Thus in America, where decisions resulting from the invitation system are counted in hundreds of thousands annually, they talk about first-time decisions because there are so many who have been to the front regularly. It was because of this particular category of people, namely those who persevered in going to the front, that pastor Norman Street, of the well known Jarvis Street Baptist Church, Toronto gave up the practice. This is how he describes his experience: 'During the first fifteen years of my ministry I gave the altar call almost every time I preached. If my message had been a moving Gospel theme, there were certain persons I knew would come forward. If it was a searching sermon on the second coming of Christ, or a sermon on heaven or on hell — it would shake them up. They would come forward, weeping and asking for prayer. They always did. I used to ask myself if these people were lost and needing to be saved. I don't know that I was ever sure. Were they backsliders needing to be restored? Who could say? Many of them never did find a resting place. They reminded me of those sad words of Paul when he said, "Ever learning and never able to come to a knowledge of the truth." That is a tragic statement. Perhaps my message would be a strong exhortation to Christians with a challenge to renounce the world and repent of un-Christlike ways. Perhaps it would be a call to prayer, or more faithfulness in giving to the Lord. In any case, I knew that as soon as the invitation was given there would be one or two men and certain women who would come forward whether anyone else did or not. They would come down the aisle under great emotion, weeping their way to the altar.

At first, I myself, as the pastor, was moved to tears because I saw in all of this encouraging evidence that the Lord was blessing the preaching of the Word. After a while it dawned on me that there was something wrong. These sincere people never did what they were always promising the Lord they would do. They talked about it, prayed about it, and wept over it, but with all the weeping and the prayers there was never any noticeable or lasting change in their behaviour or way of life. After some years of this, I became disenchanted. I began to question the wisdom of the altar call or invitation system. I continued to conclude the service in this way, though not with the same intensity. The sad thing is that some of these people to whom I refer thought of themselves as being very spiritual. Part of what they saw as proof of their spirituality was that every time the invitation was given, they came down the aisle. After all, no one can ever get too right with God, nor can anyone ever get too close to the Lord. They felt that they were always hungering and thirsting after righteousness. They felt that they were always seeking more of God. They felt that this was a sign of greater spirituality. They would even pray about others, and mention by name those they felt should have come forward. They were caught up in pure emotion and it wasn't doing anything for them.'[2]

The honest, biblical method
Ours is the technological age, when enormous harvesting machines bring in wheat or maize. There is no such thing as a parallel in the kingdom of Christ. The method he stipulated in the Great Commission is to be followed to the end of the age. We are to make disciples. A disciple is a learner. Discipling means teaching. We are so to teach that

disciples come into union with the Father, the Son and the Holy Spirit. When there is evidence of such union, then the disciples are to be baptized into the name of the Trinity (Matt. 28:18–20). Nor is that the end of the matter. They are to be taught to obey everything that Christ has commanded.

In the above testimony by pastor Norman Street we observe his longing that his ministry be blessed and prospered. That deep desire is the mark of a true gospel minister. He longs and prays for souls and labours to that end. But he knows that only God can give the increase. He cannot manufacture a harvest. Every individual who professes conversion is going to be put to the test. Those who fall away from a profession sincerely made cause great sorrow and often cause deep hurt and discouragement in a local church.

The necessity of dealing thoroughly and carefully with people individually is nowhere better illustrated than in family life. A survey of families in any church reveals much of value with regard to this subject. During the impressionable years children are all too ready to respond to an appeal and some do many times. It is essential that the necessity of discipleship be understood. Parents who are wise and discerning work overtime to ensure that their children do not put their trust in these acts of pledge, decisions or dedications. The disillusionment which was described earlier is a mortal enemy. It is desperately difficult to counsel a person who has a defeated spirit and says, 'I've tried and failed, so there is no purpose in going on.' This is precisely when there is great value and strength in a constant ministry of spiritual power and instruction. Souls are always pointed to the omnipotent God of grace, always faced with their continued responsibility. Yes, it is the tension we spoke of in chapter 2, but it is a tension which has the support of Scripture. It is biblical, whereas the 'appeal' employed as a system is artificial, misleading and harmful.

The method by which the 'appeal' is vindicated
The method used everywhere to support the public 'appeal' is by the narration of testimonies of those for whom it has worked. The pragmatic argument is most persuasive in our

day, when most people are impressed by anything that is successful. Many thrive on success stories. I have been drawing attention to the many for whom it did not work. We must not permit a success story to be blown up to such proportions for one person that the other 20, 50 or 100, for whom the decision did not work, are forgotten.

When we analyse the testimonies of those for whom it did work it is easy to see that in most cases all the discipling measures, the friendship and support of Christians and the teaching ministry were there. To the Lord, who is the author of salvation and the provider of all the means for salvation, we ascribe all the glory. For some the timing was just right with regard to their response, but surely we do not have to maintain all the machinery of the invitation system for conversions which are manifested more clearly through the appointed means of grace.

I will illustrate this by two testimonies of a husband and wife I heard recently, just before their baptism. Relating these testimonies will also illustrate my point that the method in the end proves little, because it simply becomes a contest of presenting folios of evidence for and against. At any rate, I found this one particularly instructive because the wife said that she had struggled for nine years with a bad conscience because she had made a false profession through the invitation system. It had confused her and made a hypocrite of her. She was truly glad to be free of that now. Her husband said that he welcomed the 'appeal' to which he had responded because for him it had terminated fifteen years of a bad conscience. He had longed during all that time to get a certain sin off his mind and the opportunity had never come. He saw in the invitation to go to the front a golden opportunity to have the matter dealt with.

We have just observed that you can make any position convincing by using testimonies. This one sounded as though the 'appeal' was a wonderful invention. I put the question to him: 'If a minister or sincere Bible-believing Christian had invited you personally at any time during those fifteen years, would you have responded by sharing your burden with that person?' His answer was immediate. 'Yes,' he said, 'I would have gladly responded!'

The encouragement I draw from that is that we must continue, week in and week out, with personal evangelism. We must go from house to house. I have always used this method. In that way we uncover all kinds of opportunities to help people, including the sort of need expressed by this man, who had carried his burden so long. Having discussed the issue of the 'appeal' at the personal level, we now consider the matter as it relates to churches.

2. Does the 'appeal' harm churches?

It is harmful when any church or group of churches does not conform to biblical teaching on evangelism. We should never change those teachings, tamper with them, reduce them or add to them. By adding the 'appeal' as a system, room has had to be made for thousands entering the churches who have accepted the Lord as their Saviour by a decision, even though this is not accompanied by the evidences of the new birth. For the churches to be filled with those who are not true believers is disastrous. What is this, but to serve in a direct way the interests of Satan, as is clearly seen by the parable of the wheat and tares? (Matt. 13:24–30, 36–39.)

In an effort to explain the large percentage of fall-out from evangelistic crusades, many earnest Christians have adopted a two-level theory of sanctification, called the 'carnal Christian' teaching. According to this, a person can make virtually no progress in sanctification without discovering the secret of the Spirit-filled life. Those, therefore, who make this profession of faith and thereafter show no concern for church attendance, Bible study or fellowship with the people of God are pronounced 'carnal'. They are regarded as saved souls in spite of the lack of a credible profession of faith. They are accepted as believers on the basis that they are simply unaware of the Spirit-filled life, or even, if they are aware of it, they are unwilling to claim it.

This theory teaches that carnality can be remedied in a matter of moments. One must simply recognize his sins, confess them (1 John 1:9) and then ask to be filled with the Spirit (Eph. 5:18). This filling is claimed by faith and occurs immediately, as quickly as exhaling and inhaling. Because the Word commands it, and the believer requests it, it is done. That person is now a Spirit-filled Christian. Lapses into carnality can, however, happen just as quickly. Therefore one must again go through the process of being filled with the Spirit. This in fact can happen repeatedly and can take place several times a day.

The close connection between quick, decision-centred evangelism and the development of this unbiblical view of sanctification is illustrated by the tracts put out by one of the leading college evangelistic organizations in the world, Campus Crusade for Christ. One tract, *The Four Spiritual Laws,* streamlines and stylizes a four-point evangelistic presentation so adroitly that the carefully worded appeal is virtually impossible to refuse. If it is discovered, however, that such a decision has already been made, a second tract is used teaching the person the secret of being filled with the Spirit.

The development of such a procedure and doctrine is as predictable as it is dangerous. Some explanation must be given for the number of assumed converts who apparently are not being re-created in true righteousness and holiness. It is necessary to exercise great patience in persuading the advocates of this practice to submit their thinking and methods to critical and honest examination. It is so easy to live in a self-created euphoria of success and be elated and complacent about immediate results. How tragic this is when in fact these results consist of no more than a shallow assent in response to a method which completely sidetracks the biblical demand for repentance and real faith in Christ as Lord. Many are aware that something is wrong, but are content to vindicate the method by using the 'carnal Christian' theory which I have just explained.

Perceptive leaders such as A. W. Tozer have spoken clearly on this issue. He called the practice of accepting people as believers on the basis of a decision to accept Christ as Saviour heresy! He spoke so clearly on this subject that we should give earnest attention to what he says: 'Therefore, I must be frank in my feeling that a notable heresy has come into being throughout our evangelical Christian circles — the widely-accepted concept that we humans can choose

to accept Christ only because we need Him as Saviour and
that we have the right to postpone our obedience to Him
as Lord as long as we want to!

This concept has sprung naturally from a misunderstanding
of what the Bible actually says about Christian discipleship
and obedience. It is now found in nearly all of our full
gospel literature. I confess that I was among those who
preached it before I began to pray earnestly, to study
diligently and meditate with anguish over the whole matter.

I think the following is a fair statement of what I was
taught in my early Christian experience and it certainly
needs a lot of modifying and a great many qualifiers to
save us from being in error: "We are saved by accepting
Christ as our Saviour; We are sanctified by accepting Christ
as our Lord; We may do the first without doing the second!"

The truth is that salvation apart from obedience is unknown in the sacred scriptures. Peter makes it plain that
we are "elect according to the foreknowledge of God the
Father, through sanctification of the Spirit unto obedience."

What a tragedy that in our day we often hear the gospel
appeal made on this kind of basis:

"Come to Jesus! You do not have to obey anyone. You
do not have to change anything. You do not have to give
up anything, alter anything, surrender anything, give back
anything — just come to Him and believe in Him as
Saviour!"

So they come and believe in the Saviour. Later on, in a
meeting or conference, they will hear another appeal: "Now
that you have received Him as Saviour, how would you like
to take Him as Lord?"

The fact that we hear this everywhere does not make it
right. To urge men and women to believe in a divided Christ
is bad teaching, for no one can receive half of Christ, or a
third of Christ, or a quarter of the Person of Christ! We
are not saved by believing in an office nor in a work.

I have heard well-meaning workers say, "Come and believe
on the finished work." That work will not save you. The
Bible does not tell us to believe in an office or a work, but
to believe on the Lord Jesus Christ Himself, the Person
who has done that work and holds those offices.'[3]

It is true that many churches do not practise the 'carnal

Christian' theory, as explained by A. W. Tozer. Nevertheless for reasons which have been explained throughout this book I believe the 'appeal' as a system does more harm than good. It can be argued that the constant use of 'appeals' is a reminder to the minister and the church that evangelism is paramount. Evangelism is our constant duty but it is not necessary to use a method which is not sanctioned by Scripture. It is the business of preachers to lead their flocks in personal evangelism. If they are doing this faithfully week by week they will always proclaim the whole counsel of God, and at the same time be constant, yet varied in persuading men and women of the truth of the gospel. They will do this in the same way as the apostles did and as the foremost preachers have done throughout the history of the Christian church. In the appendices which follow examples are provided. As Paul with obvious fervour and passion presented the gospel as biblical, true and reasonable, to Festus and Agrippa (Acts 26:24–29), so must we persuade men and women.

'Easy-believism' has done incalculable harm to the churches and to the testimony of Christianity. Of course, many churches have resisted the invitation system and the heresy described by Tozer, to which the system leads, but many, it would seem, have succumbed. What I have called the 'new evangelical sacrament' could, if combined with the humanism and subjectivism which pervade our Western culture, lead the professing Christian church into another dark age. We can do no better than to return to the Scriptures and make sure that the Bible is our only charter for all that we practise in evangelism.

From a positive and constructive viewpoint what can be suggested as a way ahead? Baptism is the focal point set before us in the New Testament. Modern crusade evangelism avoids this because there are different positions held by supporting churches. As we examine believers' baptism we see that it witnesses to union with the Trinity: adoption by the Father, union with Christ and the indwelling of God the Holy Spirit. The ordinance is the sign and seal of the New Covenant. God's laws have been inscribed on the believer's heart and mind (Heb. 8:10). Very clearly does believers' baptism testify to what a

Christian is and what is required for a profession of faith to be credible. Surely we should concentrate on this New Testament provision as the goal of our evangelism. We are so to preach and so to teach and counsel that it will be consistent as a result to baptize our hearers into the name of the Father, Son and Holy Spirit. The question then is not one of whether you are willing to go forward. The question is 'Are you united to the Triune God and have your sins been forgiven?' If your life supports such a testimony (Rom. 6) then the next move is obvious. It is obedience to Christ's command.[4]

Footnotes
1. Robert L. Dabney, *Discussions: Evangelical and Theological*, Banner of Truth, pp. 572—3.
2. Norman Street, *Reformation Canada.*
3. A. W. Tozer, *I call it Heresy*, Christian Publications, p. 9.
4. It is sad that circumstances have dictated that almost every book on baptism is polemical, arguing either for or against infant baptism. With apologies therefore I recommend my book on baptism as it does set out to expound the ordinance from a wholly positive position explaining what believers' baptism is designed to accomplish. *(The Testimony of Baptism,* Carey Publications.*)*

Appendix 1
Twenty-two reasons from R. T. Kendall stated and answered

R. T. Kendall in his book *Stand up and be Counted* gives twenty-two reasons why he thinks the invitation system or public pledge is a helpful practice.[1] I will give his reasons and answer them.

1. It is an appeal to the whole man
Surely it is only preaching which reaches a man in his intellect, affections, conscience and will. Does not the Scripture say that God uses the foolishness of preaching to save those who believe? The appeal does not reach the whole man. As Dr Martyn Lloyd-Jones demonstrated so clearly, it bypasses the mind.

2. It goes right against the grain of the natural man
The spirituality of the gospel, its exposure of man's sinful nature and guilt, the demands of God's holy law, the certainty of judgement to come — these truths offend the natural man. We cannot help that, but let us avoid offence coming from ourselves, our manner or our unbiblical methods (see also no. 9).

3. It temporarily takes the place of baptism
This is a remarkable admission because it contradicts the truth that we should never add anything to God's provision. Surely baptism is a perfect provision, which needs no addition or supplement?

4. It dignifies the New Testament practice of not waiting to confess after one has truly believed

The answer to this assertion follows on from the previous answer which is that in each case recorded in the New Testament it was baptism which immediately marked out the Christian. He had then to confess his faith in the world, which is much more difficult than among his friends and supporters.

5. It launches the Christian life in a very happy manner

The joy experienced at the beginning of the Christian life is one of the fruits of the Holy Spirit. To attribute the new Christian's happiness to the public pledge takes the glory away from God. In any case, there is the presumption in the original argument that the person coming forward is genuinely saved. This is frequently not the case and harm can be done which leads to anything but happiness (see chapter 11).

6. It presses home the urgency to confess Jesus Christ as Saviour and Lord

By creating an urgency not necessarily attributable to the work of the Holy Spirit, the appeal can have the effect of pressing people into a premature confession. History, experience and Scripture combine to show that urgency in evangelism relates not to the call to the front, but to the unction experienced by the preacher.

7. It provides an immediate contact with those with whom the Holy Spirit has been at work

In any normal hospitable church there is warm contact and such an artificial method should never be necessary.

8. It enables the church to know about the person most recently converted

The very nature of an evangelical church is that it works to win souls. Individuals are known personally before, during and after conversion.

9. It encourages people to bring their non-Christian friends to hear the gospel, lest their minister preach the gospel only to the converted week after week

I would certainly agree that preaching ought always to be evangelistic and to have the character of urgency, but surely we do not have to depend upon an artificial method to remind us of this. The people before us constantly remind us that they need to believe for salvation. I would far rather invite my friends to hear preaching which will persuade them to repent and believe than take them to a service where artificial pressure will be used which may well put them off permanently.

10. It lets the visitor or strangers feel that he is wanted and accepted

Both the preacher in the preaching and all the members by being friendly and hospitable should make every stranger feel welcome. Winning a friend to Christ personally makes much more sense than using a system which is confusing.

11. It visibly demonstrates the truth that all are accepted as they are

The stress here on visibility is a good one. In the early church believers were counselled for baptism. This involved visibility. Sometimes, as with Simon Magus (Acts 8), even the most able leaders can be misled. I accept that discipleship involves becoming visible, but think that the 'appeal' is an artificial method of seeking that end.

12. It gives people an opportunity to respond to what they have just heard

This suggestion raises another valuable point because it shows the need of continued contact and friendship, by which any interested person can respond and make progress. As we see from Acts 2, it is most important that spiritual life should spring from within the hearers, who asked, 'What must we do?' We want people to respond naturally and not as a result of pressure artificially applied.

13. It releases the Holy Spirit to work more freely

This is strange language because the Holy Spirit is God

omnipotent who works as he pleases. He cannot be released as though in prison. He is totally free to work as he pleases through the means he loves, namely preaching (1 Cor. 1:18).

14. It provides a further witness to those who did not go forward by those who did
This confirms our view that going forward becomes *the* issue, not repentance towards God.

15. It is a light to all the world
It is truth that constitutes light. Preaching and holy living constitute light. When those who are always learning and always responding but never changing in their lives go forward it leads to discouragement and ultimately to spiritual confusion.

16. It provides an opportunity to see the Holy Spirit at work
The book of Acts tells of the work of the Holy Spirit without a single instance of the 'appeal'.

17. It is fishing for men
Jesus said to Andrew and Peter that if they followed him he would make them fishers of men (Mark 1:17). Even fishing has rules. Fishermen must use correct methods to achieve a catch and then only take what they are going to use. For the fishing methods used by our Lord and his disciples see chapter 9.

18. It can bring life and excitement to the church
So can a wide variety of musical items, dramas, mime and exciting testimonies. The problem always is whether such life is according to truth and holiness.

19. It can bring great encouragement to the minister
It can also bring severe discouragement, especially when a careful check is kept with regard to those who persevere.

20. It goes right against Satan's chief aim
It can also be a tremendous aid to Satan, because he gains a great advantage if he can fill churches with people who are not truly born again and who rest their hope on a decision and not truly on Christ as Lord.

21. It brings rejoicing in heaven in the presence of the angels
It is not people coming to the front which brings rejoicing
in heaven but sinners coming to repentance (Luke 15:10).

22. It is honouring to God
The honour and glory of God should be our supreme aim in
all that we do. Therefore it is important that we should
study the Scriptures closely and follow the charter for
evangelism there laid out for us. We should cleave to the
methods used by our Lord and his apostles. We should not
add to those methods or compromise in any way when it
comes to the necessity of repentance towards God and
faith in our Lord Jesus Christ.

Footnotes
1.   *Stand up and be Counted*, p. 123. Published in the U.S.A. by Zondervan.

Appendix 2
Some examples of invitation preaching

The following lines record the conclusion of a sermon by R. L. Dabney and printed by the request of General 'Stonewall' Jackson, in whose presence, before a large number of soldiers, Dabney preached on the text in Ephesians 1:19, 20: 'the exceeding greatness of God's power to usward'. This is a superb example of pressing home human inability in order to shut sinners up to God, and encourage them in their responsibility to call on God for mercy.

'But I pass by this corollary, to urge upon you, in conclusion, this one solemn thought: "Except ye be born again, ye cannot see the kingdom of God." You will never work this new birth of yourselves; you are absolutely dependent on the sovereign in-working of that God against whom you sin hourly. Unless he condescends to stoop and touch your stubborn heart, it will remain ungodly, just as surely as the corpse remains dead. All the zeal of religious teachers, all your own self-righteous resolutions and vows, will be assuredly vain. But your whole life, your every act now tends to alienate that almighty hand, on whose touch your salvation depends. How complete is this dependence! How mad your rebellion! Will you not now cease fighting against your only deliverer, and begin to cry, "Create in me a clean heart, O God; and renew a right spirit within me"? (Ps. 51:10.)

I know the cavil with which impenitence excuses itself, and I know its emptiness. Will you object that my exhortation is contradictory to my doctrine? Will you tell

177

me that if you are dependent on sovereign grace, and will never change your own hearts, then the only consistent effect of the teaching must be to make you to fold your hands, and await in absolute apathy the almighty touch?

"Fold your hands," I reply, "while you passively await God's help?" Nay, your hand is stretched out every moment in active resistance to God's will and grace. Talk not to me of passivity, when the very nature of your soul is active, and that activity is ceaselessly directed by a rebellious will against God and duty. I would that you could become passive from sinning. Nor is it true that the Bible doctrine herein chills or represses your exertions after redemption; for, in truth, you do not believe in your real dependence. Would God that you did; would that you know it as well as I do, for then we should see you, instead of coldly cavilling against facts and duty and grace, crying mightily unto God for his aid. It is not according to reason or nature that your clear knowledge of your coming ruin, and of your absolute dependence on help from above for deliverance, should paralyse effort or produce apathy. Here is a man whose house is hopelessly involved in flames. He is within, in an upper chamber, busily collecting his treasures, and he supposes that he has the means of escape wholly at his own command, to resort to them whenever he deemed it imprudent to venture farther. This notion, as you well know, will tempt him to postpone his escape, to venture near the utmost moment, to listen to the attractions of his wealth which he would fain rescue.

And this is just your delusion now. But meantime the man casually looks at the stairway without, by which he expected to escape, and finds to his surprise that it is wrapped in flames. He sees that he has no means of egress at his own command; unless assistance comes from without he is lost. Now, what does nature or reason prompt this man to do? That moment there is an end of his rash delays. No longer does he tamper with the rescue; his dearest treasures drop from his hands, and he runs to a window and shouts, "Help, help, or I am gone!"

So do you cry to God. It is the very thing, the only thing, which a helpless sinner, who is guilty for his very helplessness, should do. "Save, Lord, or I perish!" ' [1]

C. H. Spurgeon reasoned with, urged, invited, implored,
entreated and commanded his hearers to repent and believe
the gospel. The following example is from a sermon on
Isaiah 1:18 (sermon 366).
'Come now. Mortal man so near thy end — thus saith the
Lord, "Set thy house in order, for thou shalt die and not
live; and because I will do this, consider your ways." Come
now. Oh, that I had power to send home this invitation!
But it must be left in the Master's hands. Yet, if an anxious
heart could do it, how would I plead with you! Sinner, is
hell so pleasant that thou must needs endure it? Is heaven
a trifle that thou must needs lose it? What? Is the wrath of
God which abideth on thee no reason why thou shouldest
labour to escape? What? Is not a perfect pardon worth the
having? Is the precious blood of Christ worthless? Is it
nothing to thee that the Saviour should die? Man, art thou
a fool? Art thou mad? If thou must needs play the fool
go and sport with thy gold and silver, but not with thy
soul.

Be wise, man. O, Spirit of God, make this sinner wise!
We may preach, but it is thine to apply. Lord apply it.
Come forth great Spirit. Come from the four winds, O
breath, and breathe upon these slain that they may live.
In the name of Jesus of Nazareth, O, Spirit of God come
forth! By the voice that once bade the winds cease from
roaring, and the waves lie still, come thou Spirit of the
living God! In the name of Jesus who was crucified,
sinners, believe and live. I preach not now in my own
name, or in my own strength, but in the name of him who
gave himself for sinners on the cross. "Repent and be baptized every one of you." "Believe on the Lord Jesus Christ
and ye shall be saved".'

Thomas Brooks repudiates the necessity of special quali-
fications, using Revelation 3:20 in particular.
'The remedy against the device of Satan that they lack
preparation is solemnly to dwell upon these following
Scriptures, which do clearly evidence that poor sinners
which are not so and so prepared and qualified to meet
with Christ, to receive and embrace the Lord Jesus Christ,
may, notwithstanding that, believe in Christ, and rest and

lean upon him for happiness and blessedness, according to
the gospel. Read Proverbs 1:20–33, and chapter 8:1–11,
and chapter 9:1–6; Ezekiel 16:1–14; John 3:14–18;
Revelation 3:15–20. Here the Lord Jesus Christ stands
knocking at the Laodiceans' door; he would fain have them
to sup with him, and that he might sup with them; that is
that they might have intimate communion and fellowship
one with another.

Now, pray tell me, what preparations or qualifications
had these Laodiceans to entertain Christ? Surely none;
for they were lukewarm, they were "neither hot nor cold",
they were "wretched, and miserable and poor, and blind,
and naked", and yet Christ, to shew his free grace and his
condescending love, invites the very worst of sinners to
open to him, though they were no ways so and so prepared
or qualified to entertain him.'[2]

*John Flavel presents the case of tendered mercy and goes
on to show the awful danger of rejecting Christ's offer, using
the same text (Rev. 3:20).*
'1. Consider how invaluable it is that you are yet within the
reach of offered mercy. What vast tracts are there where
Christ is unknown!
2. Consider the nature, weight and worth of the mercies
which this day are freely offered you. Christ the first-born
of mercies, and in him pardon, peace and eternal salvation
are set before you.
3. Consider who it is that makes these gracious tenders of
pardon, peace and salvation, to you — even that God whom
you have so deeply wronged, whose laws you have violated,
whose mercies you have spurned and whose wrath you have
justly incensed. God intreats you to be reconciled (2 Cor.
5:20).'[3]

*Richard Sibbes wrests excuses from those to whom mercy
is offered in expounding Luke 2:13, 14.*
'And consider how God offers this in the gospel, and lays
a command . . . Thou questionest whether thou be one that
Christ died for or no? Believe in him, and obey him, and
thou puttest that question out of the question. Thou doubt-
est whether God love thee or no? Cast thyself upon the love

of God in Christ, and then it is out of question. Whosoever
hath grace to cast himself upon the free love of God, he
fulfils the covenant of grace. Stand not disputing and
wrangling, but desire grace to obey; and then all questions
concerning thy eternal estate are resolved; all is clear.'[4]

It would be appropriate to include a contemporary example.
Preaching has been dominated by concepts of human ability.
God has often been pictured as poor and powerless and the
wicked as sovereign masters to do with the Almighty as
they please. This had led to an unhealthy over-caution on
the part of some who have come to appreciate the biblical
truth of free grace.
A modern example: Ezekiel 18:31 Conclusion of sermon.
'From the context we see then that the children of Israel
were blaming God for the mess they were in. They were in
Babylon under God's judgement. But God would not accept
the blame. They were to blame. The fault and the responsibility were theirs. Their hearts were hard and unrepentant.
God said to them that it was their responsibility to turn
and make themselves new hearts. If they did not they would
die!

Here we are in this age when men visit the moon — an age
of science and technology when men are arrogant and think
they know everything, but we too are in captivity. We are
slaves of sin and we are under the judgement of God.
Violence, adultery and lies are as rife now as ever. Out of
the heart of man proceeds a squalid flow of filth and blasphemy. The heart stands for the man himself; the fountain
of his life; the spring of his disposition, thoughts and actions.
If it is not changed the consequences are terrifying, since it
will go on producing sin and accruing the wrath of God.
Finally the whole man, body and soul, will be banished
into everlasting fire.

What about your heart? Are you a slave of lust? Are you
ungodly? "Yes!" you retort. "I am, and I side with those
Israelites in captivity. It is preposterous to say I must change
my heart! Have you not said that only God can do that?
Have you not been saying that God gives repentance and
faith? Have you not just said that only God quickens? You
said just now that regeneration belongs to God. Now you
tell me I must change my own heart!"

Yes! Absolutely! You are to change your own heart! By that I mean that the full weight of responsibility for what you are by nature as a sin-lover rests upon you. You are responsible to change your own heart. You are to do works meet for repentance. That means you are to make full use of the means God has provided for you.

The Bible, preaching, contact with believers — full use is to be made of these. But mainly you are to make you a new heart, by placing yourself under preaching. The Scripture says that faith comes by hearing the Word of God. And here you are under that very preaching. And the best part of that preaching is Jesus Christ. He is here and he says to you, "Come to me." Yes, as you are, you are to come. He will change your heart. Everything you need will be found in him. He invites you to come now. His transforming work is offered to you. Dr Barnard, the heart-transplant surgeon, may offer a dying man a new organ, but it will soon wear out. Here the Great Physician, even the eternal and all powerful Son of God, promises to do all for you. That which you can never do for yourself, he will do. I beseech you to call on him immediately and ask him to be your Saviour and your Physician.

Now you see you are under a greater responsibility than before. You cannot plead inability as your excuse. To turn away from him who is the resurrection and the life when he is within arm's reach is sheer madness. You must not do it. You cannot do it for to do that is to sentence yourself to eternal damnation. You do not want to weep for ever. Yet your hell will be made worse by regret that you turned your back on the Prince of life. It is not to me you come. It is not to a counsellor. It is not to a priest. It is not to a special enquiry room. You do not have to move one inch. You do not have to raise your hand. You do not have to stand. Right there where others have received a new heart you may call upon the Lord, as the Scripture says: "Seek ye the Lord while he may be found, call ye upon him while he is near." You make you a new heart by looking to him. May he bless you and change you, now and for evermore, for his name's sake. Amen.'

We conclude by observing how John Bunyan followed Peter in addressing sinners.

Bunyan in his sermon on Luke 24:47, 'The Jerusalem sinner saved or Good News for the Vilest of Men', draws out several reasons why mercy should be offered to the biggest sinners.

'1. Jesus Christ would have mercy offered to the biggest sinners because they have the most need thereof. 2. Offered to the biggest sinners because when they, any of them, receive it, it redounds most to the fame of his name. 3. Offered to the biggest sinners, because they, when converted will love him most. 4. Offered to the biggest sinners because by their forgiveness and salvation, others, hearing of it will be encouraged the more to come to him for life.'

Bunyan sets his nets to catch the biggest sinners and makes sure that they are included when mercy is to be offered.

'*Objection.* But I have a heart as hard as a rock.

Answer. Well, but this doth but prove thee a biggest sinner.

Objection. But my heart continually frets against the Lord.

Answer. Well, this doth but prove thee a biggest sinner.

Objection. But I have been desperate in sinful courses.

Answer. Well, stand thou with the number of the biggest sinners.

Objection. But my grey head is found in the way of wickedness.

Answer. Well, thou art in the rank of the biggest sinners.

Objection. But I have not only a base heart, but I have lived a debauched life.

Answer. Stand thou also among those that are called the biggest sinners.'

Finally he removes all excuses from the biggest sinners:

'Repent, every one of you; be baptized, every one of you, in his name, for the remission of sins, and you shall, every one of you, receive the gift of the Holy Ghost.

Obector. But I was one of them that plotted to take away his life. May I be saved by him?

Peter. Every one of you.

Objector. But I was one of them that bare false witness against him. Is there grace for me?

Peter. For every one of you.

Objector. But I was one of them that cried out, "Crucify him, crucify him," and desired that Barabbas, the murderer, might live, rather than him. What will become of me, think you?

Peter. I am to preach repentance and remission of sins to every one of you.

Objector. But I was one of them that did spit in his face when he stood before his accusers. I also was one that mocked him, when in anguish he hanged bleeding on the tree. Is there room for me?

Peter. For every one of you.

Objector. But I was one of them that, in his extremity, said, "Give him gall and vinegar to drink." Why may not I expect the same when anguish and guilt is upon me?

Peter. Repent of these your wickednesses, and here is remission of sins for every one of you.

Objector. But I railed on him, I reviled him, I hated him, I rejoiced to see him mocked at by others. Can there be hope for me?

Peter. There is, for every one of you. Repent, and be baptized every one of you in the name of Jesus Christ, for the remission of sins, and ye shall receive the gift of the Holy Ghost.

Oh, what a blessed "every one of you" is here! How willing was Peter, and the Lord Jesus, by his ministry, to catch these murderers with the word of the gospel, that they might be made monuments of the grace of God! How unwilling, I say, was he, that any of these should escape the hand of mercy! Yea, what an amazing wonder is it to think, that above all the world, and above everybody in it, these should have the first offer of mercy! Beginning at Jerusalem.'[5]

Here is universality. Here is application of the gospel to the biggest sinners. Here is a rich example of what it is to offer the gospel the free grace way. May we twentieth-century preachers go and do likewise.

Footnotes
1. *Discussions,* vol. 1, p. 482 ff.
2. *Works,* vol. 1, p. 146.
3. *Works,* vol. 4, p. 26 ff. Flavel's exposition on Revelation 3:20, 'Behold, I stand at the door and knock!' extends to 258 pages. Magnificent!
4. *Works,* vol. 6, p. 354.
5. *Works,* vol. 1, pp. 71 and 88.

Lightning Source UK Ltd.
Milton Keynes UK
07 October 2009

144672UK00001B/24/A